Storybook Weddings

A Guide to Fun and Romantic Theme Weddings

by Robin Kring

 **Meadowbrook Press**

Distributed by Simon & Schuster
New York

Library of Congress Cataloging-in-Publication Data
Kring, Robin.
    Storybook weddings: a guide to fun and romantic theme weddings/
    by Robin Kring.
        p. cm.
    ISBN 0-88166-353-0 (Meadowbrook)
    ISBN 0-671-31654-0 (Simon & Schuster)
    1. Weddings—Planning. 2. Wedding etiquette. I. Title.
    BJ2051.K737   1998
    395.2'2—dc21   98-47203
                                                                      CIP

Editor: Liya Lev Oertel
Production Manager: Joe Gagne
Production Assistant: Danielle White
Cover Photo: Kevin Lein
Illustrations: Michael Crampton

Published by Meadowbrook Press, 5451 Smetana Drive, Minnetonka,
Minnesota 55343

BOOK TRADE DISTRIBUTION by Simon & Schuster, a division of Simon
and Schuster, Inc., 1230 Avenue of the Americas, New York, NY 10020

03 02 01 00 99   10 9 8 7 6 5 4 3 2 1

Printed in the United States of America

Dedication

To Michael, My Handsome Prince,
Whose Essence of Romance Inspires Me Daily

Acknowledgments

Thank you to the many brides and event planners who shared their storybook dreams and ideas with me. A special thank you to Peggy Hazelwood, whose supportive friendship and technical expertise has helped me become a better writer. To Bruce Lansky, thank you for giving me the opportunity to put these wedding tales in print. And to Liya Lev Oertel, my editor, thank you for polishing my writing to such a pretty shine. Finally, an affectionate thank you to my mom and dad, who gave me the love and confidence to pursue these storybook dreams.

Table of Contents

Introduction

Open this book to find everything you'll need to design a storybook wedding (handsome prince not included). Theme weddings are quickly becoming the hottest new wedding trend. Today's bride and groom are choosing to stretch the rules of tradition with unique romantic ambiance. Whether you are planning a small, intimate affair or a spectacular wedding extravaganza, a theme wedding is a very romantic expression of love.

Storybook Weddings offers wedding themes based on romantic history, such as a Wedding Breakfast in Camelot or a Victorian Wedding Tea; popular holidays, such as Love in Any Language (A Valentine Wedding) or Dreaming of a White Wedding (A Christmas Romance); exciting scenic locations, such as Wedding on the Orient Express and Arabian Nights (A Wedding of Middle Eastern Mystique), and many, many more. Whether you are looking for fun, romance, or excitement, *Storybook Weddings* has a theme for you.

Use as many or as few of the suggestions as you like: Follow all the suggestions to create an elaborate storybook romance—a real affair to remember—or use only a few suggestions to add sparkle and pizzazz to your traditional wedding plans.

Romance lies between the pages of this book. Now, turn the page to find your "happily ever after" storybook wedding.

Chapter One

How to Plan a Theme Wedding

T heme weddings are modern interpretations of age-old traditional weddings. Family, friends, religious leaders, and wedding vendors are all familiar and comfortable with traditional weddings. Therefore, you will have to use care and consideration when you communicate your novel ideas to everyone involved. For instance, unique themes may take a little explaining. Grandma may not understand that "calypsoing" in the Caribbean is actually a creative way to celebrate a wedding in Mom and Dad's backyard.

Choosing a Theme

As with any other event, choose a theme for your wedding that *you* think will be romantic and fun. You will not be able to please everyone, so you shouldn't try. The themes in this book are unique in design, yet take practical application and guests' comfort into account. So, if you are happy and enthusiastic about the theme you have chosen, you will find that your guests will share your enthusiasm and enjoy your celebration.

The key to a wedding theme's success is its application. The wedding theme should compliment the wedding occasion—not overpower the wedding couple or the true meaning of the day. Make the bridal couple the center of attention. You don't want guests to become so caught up in the decorations and the activities that they forget they are at a wedding.

Invitations

To help explain your theme wedding, enclose a personalized note with your invitations. Explain that you have chosen to exchange your wedding vows and celebrate the wedding reception with creative flair. Include your telephone number, along with one or two numbers of an informed friend or family member. Invite the guest to call with any questions he or she might have.

Consider including a short description of the reception meal or refreshments on the reception card insert. This is an especially good idea if you are providing anything other than a standard dinner. For example, write, "You are invited to a cake and champagne reception," "Dinner reception at six o'clock in the evening," "An old-fashioned pancake breakfast will be served immediately following the ceremony," "Cocktails and hors d'oeuvres will be served at the reception," and so on. Be sure to consider the time of your reception when you choose your menu—a full meal is appropriate at dinner time, while "hors d'oeuvres only" menus and cake and champagne receptions are appropriate for late afternoon (before dinner) or evening (after dinner).

I suggest that you also include suggestions for appropriate attire, on the insert or directly on the invitation. This is a variance to strict etiquette rules, which approve listing "Black Tie" and other suggestions on *party* invitations, but not on formal *wedding* invitations. Traditionally, the event's scheduled time dictated the attire.

Over the years, strict etiquette rules have relaxed, and some have even been ignored. Nonetheless, theme weddings are a pioneering effort and, therefore, may generate some controversial changes to traditional etiquette guidelines, such as unsual wording on a wedding invitation. However, today's brides' growing desires for creative weddings indicate a trend toward acceptance of "bending the etiquette" rules, while still exercising good taste and consideration for one's guests. Providing information to guests, even in this modern and creative way, is an act of curtesy—the true essence of correct etiquette.

To avoid any confusion, consider forming a calling circle to follow up on unique invitations. Allow a reasonable time for receipt of invitations, then call each guest to ask whether he or she has received the wedding invitation. This will also give guests a chance to ask any questions, if they are curious. When recruiting your calling circle, make sure each caller is informed and enthusiastic about the theme.

Remember to properly pack any items you enclose with the invitations, and to attach the proper postage. Consult your local Post Office or overnight carrier if you have questions about packaging or postage. There may be some restrictions on sending food items. Although, technically, you can even send an unwrapped tennis shoe through the mail, you may want to box it to ensure against damage. Consider having unique invitations hand delivered. Hire a courier service or a team of reliable high-school or college students.

Requesting Guests to Wear Costumes

Guests may feel a little uneasy about wearing costumes or any unusual attire. That's all right. Don't force the issue. Encourage guests to participate at their own comfort level. You might include the word "optional" under requests for special attire. Or, let guests know, *if they ask,* that traditional wedding attire is also appropriate. A diplomatic reply to any costume-related question is, "I hope all guests will dress according to the theme, however I don't want the dress requirement to keep anyone from attending. After all, we're looking forward to sharing our special day with our family and friends."

Wedding-Party Dress and Theme Decor

View the wedding party's dress and the site decor as an *interpretation* of the theme, not as an exact re-creation of the time period or event. Don't be obsessed with being perfectly authentic. The goal should be to take inspiration from the theme, not to re-create it exactly. This flexibility will make planning, shopping, and executing the wedding event a lot easier.

Comfort is an important factor to consider. You may not actually want to re-create the wedding costume exactly as it once was. For example, do you really want to wear the stiff, uncomfortable underclothes all women wore at the turn of the century? Or, do you want to suffer in the tight leg girdles and pointed bras of the 1950s? Consider that authentic Cinderella glass slippers may pinch, and an authentic royal crown may be a bit expensive.

Mix twentieth-century comfort with authentic designs. Don't be afraid to use theatrical props instead of the real thing. You'll probably find a prop "royal crown" to be closer to your budget's price range. And a fake Prince's sword will be safer. Perhaps reclining on couches while eating—for the Roman design—is impractical and expensive. That's all right. Plan for traditional banquet tables and chairs instead. Is custom-made theme decor for the reception room out of your budget? Then concentrate on providing theme centerpieces for guest tables.

Will the groom feel extremely silly in tights? Substitute a pair of slim slacks. Would you rather wear silk than period-authentic heavy brocade? That's okay. Go with your preference.

When planning wedding-party dress, consider the wedding's date. Heavy, long-sleeved gowns may seem appealing in the winter, but if the wedding is scheduled for the middle of the hot summer, you may want to reconsider your choice—especially if the ceremony will take place in a non-air-conditioned facility.

Finally, I would like to offer two very important tips that experience has taught me. The first is to take extra care in final fittings, and again when you pick up the formal wear. During the fittings, always wear the exact shoes and undergarments planned for the wedding day. Keep in mind that although the gown may fit when you are standing straight and tall, you're likely to find that the gown is just a hair too long when you assume your normal posture. Take the time to walk in your gown, to make sure you can do so comfortably, without tripping. Also, bend normally and try sitting in the gown. Do this at the final fitting, as well as when you go to pick up the gown. If you notice any needed alterations at the wedding site, it will be too late. Also, encourage the groom and his groomsmen to try on tuxes and shoes when they pick them up. People tend to assume that because they have been measured, everything will fit perfectly. This is not true. Take the extra time and effort to ensure comfort on the special day.

The second tip I have learned is simply to wear comfortable shoes. No matter how wonderful or beautiful the shoes are, uncomfortable shoes will spoil the event. Have your dress designer embellish a pair of comfortable shoes to match your ensemble. Wear these shoes before the wedding and really break them in. You can always touch up scuff marks.

Coordinating Wedding Vendors

When visiting a proposed site, florist, photographer, caterer, baker, or other vendor, tell them about your wedding theme. First, ask them for any ideas they may have to complement the theme. Then, tell them what you have in mind. Listen to their opinions, comments, and suggestions.

Once you have vendor contracts in place, follow up consistently. If your plan has any unusual elements, gentle reminders will help the vendors to remember those special details. Perhaps they will have to place special orders or prepare special products and services.

The key to any successful event is careful planning—follow up, follow up, and then follow up again. I suggest following up in writing, as well as in person or by phone.

Finally, I share some important advice that I *always* use professionally and personally. Plan and coordinate every detail thoroughly and completely, but expect that some of your plans may not turn out as planned —and accept this. Don't let a minor, or for that matter, a major detail spoil your special day. Don't let it bother you. You did the best that you could. And probably no one will even notice it. Even if something disastrous happens, like Santa's reindeer eats all the prime rib when you're not looking, make the best of it. Order pizza, and consider it something to laugh about in later years.

Working with Clergy

Be sure to check with the person who will be officiating at your wedding about your planned theme. He or she might have some objections to your planned ceremony. For instance, the Catholic church has recently prohibited its priests from conducting ceremonies at Walt Disney World's Cinderella Palace.

If any part of your plan is objectionable, try to change or omit it, and work to reach a satisfactory compromise. If you are unable to reach a compromise, don't despair; plan a traditional religious ceremony, and concentrate your theme entirely on the wedding reception.

Hiring a Wedding Coordinator

Now that you have carefully planned your theme wedding, consider the on-site coordination efforts. Any event, including a wedding, takes hours of careful prewedding planning and coordination. It also takes attentive and experienced on-site coordination efforts. Weddings, in the past, were traditionally coordinated by the bride's mother, or even a caterer or professional wedding coordinator. Today, many brides and grooms plan and coordinate their own weddings. Couples marry when they are older, and many pay for their own weddings. Even in parent-sponsored weddings, the bride and groom choose to take a more active role in the planning and organization.

Planning a theme wedding is a lot like directing an elaborate stage production. When planning, imagine the wedding and reception from the beginning to end. Think through each and every detail. Will the site allow you to light kerosene lanterns for your western-theme centerpieces? Does the fire marshal require that all decor be fire retardant? Are the rings secured to the unique ring pillow? Can they be easily removed? Imagine the entire process, from the moment the wedding site doors open until the bride and groom leave for the honeymoon. Then, you'll have to plan for cleanup and vacating the site.

Even if the bride and groom choose to organize all prewedding details, I strongly suggest delegating on-site coordination responsibilities. Arrange for an experienced family member or a professional wedding coordinator or event planner to handle on-site details. The reason is simple. It will free the bridal couple from wedding day interruptions and details. At the very least, hire or designate an experienced person to coordinate the entertainment and theme activities, such as leading the treasure hunt or coordinating the bagpipe players with the harpist. The coordinator has to know how to let people participate at their own comfort level. Designating an experienced person to coordinate the activities will ensure success. It will also allow the bride and groom to concentrate on their wedding day and to really enjoy the special celebration.

That is what this unique theme wedding celebration is all about. It's about pledging life-long love to one another. Enjoy and share in the time spent together planning for this special event. Treasure your wedding vows, and take delight in the romantic ambiance of your storybook event, which will mark the beginning of a lifetime together.

Chapter Two

Complete Wedding Theme Designs

Wedding Breakfast in Camelot

The fictional story of King Arthur's Camelot and his love for Guineviere is set during the end of the Middle Ages, after the medieval era and before the Renaissance. When recreating details from a particular era, you will find influences of the preceding as well as following eras. Also, remember that you don't have to recreate each detail exactly. All details, including clothing and decorations, should reflect the mood of the era, while allowing for artistic interpretation. As in any time period, this era has more than one style of dress and decor. Make decisions according to your personal likes and dislikes, comfort, availability, and budget. Don't be afraid to alter the suggestions below or to add some ideas of your own. After all, as temporary King and Queen of the new Camelot, your royal proclamation is sovereign.

Invitations

- Send guests a reproduction of a medieval scroll, inviting them to "Celebrate This Fairy-Tale Romance with a Wedding Breakfast in Camelot." To make the scroll invitations, roll a piece of parchment paper into a tube-like shape, seal with a wax seal, and stamp the seal with an insignia—the couple's initials, a heart, or a castle. Tie the scrolls with a satin or velvet ribbon—royal blue, scarlet, purple, or gold.

- Use Old English phrases to compose the invitation. Write it using one of these methods:

  —Have a calligrapher pen each scroll (this would be pricey).

  —Produce the invitations on a personal computer using a calligraphic font.

  —Find a stationer who offers calligraphy printing machine services.

  —Have a printing company print the invitations using an Old English script font.

Guests' Dress

As in the Middle Ages, have the royal couple (bride and groom) choose a royal color. Enclose a separate note with the invitations, requesting all royal guests to wear clothing in the chosen color. (Be sure that the guests' color is not the same as the bride's.)

Wedding-Party Dress

Bride

- Rent or buy a costume from a costume company, or have a wedding gown custom-designed to resemble an English fourteenth-century wedding gown. Use the movies *First Knight* or *Camelot* as your inspiration, and consider these clothing details:

  —A popular style of gown in this era was the coteharide, a close-fitting gown with a scoop neck, long, tight-fitting sleeves, full skirt starting just below the hip-line, and an extremely long train attached at the shoulders.

  —Royal wedding gowns were generally white satin, embroidered with silver and precious gems and often trimmed with fur. However, today's bride may prefer simpler embellishments.

  —From the fourteenth to early seventeenth century, the bride tradition-ally wore her hair hanging down her back as a sign of her virginity. Today's bride might find a jewel-decorated braid or a flower-trimmed coiffure a romantic alternative to this custom.

  —Bejeweled crowns worn by royalty in this time period can be easily duplicated.

Bridal Bouquet

Substitute a small white Bible for the modern bridal bouquet at this Camelot wedding.

Groom

Dress the groom in knee-length tunic, pants covered by knee-high leather boots, and a long, flowing cape-robe (as depicted in the movie *First Knight*).

This regal and sophisticated ensemble will appeal to today's groom more than the traditional hose or breeches worn during this time period. Choose bright blue or scarlet velvet fabrics with black trim. Complete the costume with a crown and an arm shield (decorated with a royal crest).

Groomsmen

Dress the groomsmen similarly to the groom, in knee-length tunics and pants covered by knee-high leather boots. Eliminate the cape, but add the arm shield and a coronet (a smaller or lesser crown signifying a rank lower than that of a sovereign).

Bridesmaids

- Choose silver gowns similar to the bride's coteharide, but without the train.
- Adorn the bridesmaids' hair similarly to the bride's, and add a coronet.
- Have the bridesmaids carry the bride's train down the wedding aisle, and have one maid wrap the end of the train over her arm during the ceremony.

Flower Girl

Children weren't included in these ancient wedding ceremonies, but including a flower girl in a modern-day version is easy:

- Dress the girl in a gown similar to the bridesmaids', and add a Renaissance-style hat, the henin (a tall cone-shaped hat with a veil at its tip).
- Have the flower girl spread rosemary and fragrant petals along the bridal path.

Ring Bearer

- Dress the ring bearer as a page, in a tunic with a short cape and hose (tights).
- Add ballet-style or velvet slippers and a velvet chaperon (a floppy, oversized, tam-like hat).
- Give the ring bearer a rolled scroll tied with a ribbon, and attach the wedding rings to the ribbon.

Ceremony

Wedding Site

Choose a gothic-style church for a formal ceremony. For a less formal wedding, hold the ceremony in a meadow. In this case, set up separate bride and groom tents for dressing and last minute adjustments.

Decor

- Have guardsmen form a tunnel with swords for the wedding processional.
- Costume the guardsmen in tunics covered with a breastplate, tight slacks with knee-high leather boots and knee caps, and gauntlets for the arms. Add a helmet to complete the look.
- Line the aisle with torches placed in tall iron stands.
- Hang flower garlands on pew sides or other seating.
- Set up ornate candelabras at the alter.

Music

Hire bagpipe musicians to lead the wedding processional.

Special Touches

- Announce the royal couple with a bugle call or a trumpet flare.
- Shoot a confetti cannon to shower the royal couple as they leave the church or wedding vow area.

Transportation

Arrange for a horse and carriage to take the royal couple to the reception. If the bride and groom are experienced equestrians, have them ride white horses decorated with flowers and royal banners (side-saddle for the bride).

Reception

Area Decor

Hold the reception in a meadow, or transform a hall or ballroom into a romantic Camelot:

- Frame the entrance with shining suits of armor. Better yet, costume two actors as knights wearing suits of armor to greet guests at the entrance. (If holding the event outdoors, place the knights on white horses.)

- Hang a castle backdrop on a focal-point wall—behind the royal table or on the stage.
- Decorate the room with black iron candleholders and coat-of-arm shields.
- Dress greeters as court jesters, and waitstaff in period commoner costumes. Encourage the waitstaff and entertainment to act out their parts, offering curtsies and proper royal greetings, such as "Your Majesty."

Table Decor

Seat the bridal party and guests at round banquet tables decorated with a "Knights of the Round Table" theme:

- Cover tables with black tablecloths, and cover chairs with black chair covers and silver cord sashes.
- Hang feather-plumed knight-costume helmets on the backs of chairs. Choose a different-colored feather plume for each table, and use the colors for table-seating assignments.
- Lay silver-colored swords (costume or foam board) at each place setting, from the table's edge to its center.
- Add a flaming centerpiece made with a cast-iron bowl of lit coals or candles.
- Set out pewter or silver goblets for the bride and groom, or a Coup de Marriage—a two-handled wedding goblet.

Favors

Wedding favors were given to all connected to the wedding ceremony— the most popular being gloves, scarves, and ribbon decorations. The ribbon decorations were known as bride laces and knots. The bride wore the ribbons during the wedding, and later cut them into little pieces and distributed to guests. Today, consider giving these Camelot-inspired favors:

- Ribbon-rose decorations made into magnets, brooches, or napkin rings
- Silver or pewter goblets, engraved with "Wedding in Camelot"
- Small flasks of mead, a type of honey wine dating back to the Middle Ages (Traditionally, the father of the bride supplied his son-in-law with mead for a month after the wedding. Because of the lunar-based calendar, the period was called the "honey month"—what we call today the "honeymoon.")
- Rosemary herb sachets or sprigs dipped in gold paint and tied with ribbon (Rosemary is the symbol of remembrance and fidelity. In the

Middle Ages, this gift signified that the wedding couple would never forget the friends and family they were leaving behind. See Supplier Resource Directory, page 165.)

Tip: Dress children as pages, and have them distribute purple, velvet bags filled with foil-wrapped coins. Attach a note reading, "In honor of the wedding, the king has rescinded taxes for the day."

Guest Book

Place a large scroll and quill pen at the entrance, to serve as the royal guest book.

Entertainment

- Hold a jousting tournament.
- Hire strolling jesters, magicians (perhaps King Arthur's Merlin), jugglers, minstrels, and musicians (mandolin, hammer-dulcimer, bagpipe, and harp). Ask them to dress in Renaissance-period costumes.
- Set up an archery range.
- Hold a bride's garter tournament: Have the available bachelors use swords (costume or toy) to catch the garter.
- Play a chess game with human chess pieces: Use the bride and groom for the King and Queen, and costumed guests or actors for the other pieces. If playing outside, have the knights sit on actual horses.

Menu

Even though this is a wedding "breakfast," it's really a banquet that is served early in the day. Serve huge piles of everything, on very large platters:

- Roast pig, smoked salmon, venison, hearty roast, steaming stew, and crusty hot meat pies
- Bread, rolls, cheese, and fruit
- Ales, wines, mead, and royal punch

Cake

- Choose a large and majestic cake—possibly depicting a castle or a knight on a horse.
- Have the bride and groom cut the cake with a prop sword—wrap the handle with flowing satin ribbons. (If using a real sword, be careful, and be sure to keep it out of children's reach.)

"Do as the Romans Do" Wedding Feast

"When in Rome . . . do as the Romans do." Invite guests to celebrate your wedding in ancient Roman tradition. The Roman wedding ceremony and feast were elaborate and indulgent, planned for uniting empires and fortunes. Today, this wedding theme lends itself equally well to informal and formal celebrations. Although some Roman traditions (reclining on couches to dine, eating with the hands, and so on) may be awkward for a formal wedding celebration, they may be fun for an informal, possibly second, wedding. Whether you plan an elaborately decorated wedding celebration, or whether you just borrow a few Roman theme ideas, this theme will envelope you and your guests in Romanesque romance.

Invitations

Invite friends and family to "celebrate with the bride and groom in the ancient city of love" with one of these unique invitation ideas:

- Enclose a map or postcard of Rome with each invitation.
- Deliver a miniature bust of Caesar or a laurel wreath with each invitation.
- Inscribe details on a parchment scroll, tie with a satin or velvet ribbon, and seal each scroll with a wax stamp—use a heart framing the couple's initials.
- Enclose a cloth napkin with each invitation, and attach a note explaining the following Roman custom: Ancient Roman guests usually brought their own napkins to the celebration, later filling them with leftover food to take home. You may want to use Photonaps—napkins printed with a photo of the bride and groom. These napkins are available commercially.

Guests' Dress

Include a note with each invitation asking guests to wrap themselves in togas to join the "Romance in Rome" celebration.

Wedding-Party Dress

Bride

- Make an excellent Roman statement with a floor-length toga (a long, sleeveless, chiffon column gown). Choose a wedding-white material with gold-trim finish and a braided cord crisscrossing the bodice and circling the waist. Or, trim the dress with purple bands, as did ancient magistrates and other officials. Add a translucent, flowing train.

- If you prefer, create or choose a toga in the royal color of red or gold.

- Cover the bride's train with a light blanket of flowers.

- Add ankle-strapped sandals and a gold laurel wreath as a headpiece to complete the bride's ensemble.

Bridal Bouquet

Follow an old Roman wedding custom to ward off evil spirits—carry a bouquet of herbs. Or, carry a fragrant, picturesque bouquet of lilac.

Groom

- Match one of the following toga designs to the bride's ensemble:
  - Floor-length white Doric tunic with gold or purple trim (This tunic is made with a single large piece of material, draped around the body and fastened at the right shoulder and side. The top of the material is folded over the chest to form a bib, draping nearly to the waist.)
  - Toga in the royal color of red or gold
  - Short tunic with a braided cord sash
- Add leather sandals and a wreath headpiece of gold laurel to complete the ensemble.

Groomsmen

Dress groomsmen in short tunics worn just above the knee, and add Roman soldier armor costume pieces over the tunic. To complete the ensemble, add a helmet and leather sandals.

Bridesmaids

- Make gold-brocade, floor-length togas.
- Add ankle-strap sandals and dried-flower-wreath headpieces.
- Have the bridesmaids carry the bride's train or single stalks of wheat during the wedding processional.

Flower Girl

- Dress the flower girl in a short, gold-brocade toga, and add sandals and a dried-flower-wreath headpiece.
- Have the flower girl carry a conch shell filled with scented rose water to dribble along the bridal path.

Ring Bearer

- Dress the ring bearer in a short tunic toga with braided cord sash, sandals, and a gold-laurel-wreath headpiece.
- Have the ring bearer carry an ornate, but light, handled ceramic or metal vase. Tie the wedding rings to one of the handles.

Ceremony

Wedding Site

Hold the wedding ceremony in a park, at an Italian restaurant, or in a Romanesque-architecture facility (city park, library, and so on). Or transform a backyard, hotel ballroom, or banquet site into the ancient city of love.

Decor

- Hang garlands of myrtle sprig (a lovely, evergreen, bushy shrub with oval and lance-shaped shiny leaves, fragrant white or rosy flowers, and black berries).
- Drape a myrtle-sprig garland between two Roman columns to serve as the wedding arch.
- Use Roman pillars to form an aisle for the wedding procession.

- Decorate the area with ivy, reflecting pools, stone columns, urns, and a bronze sundial.
- Add life-sized copies of Roman art statues, busts of Caesar, wall torches, fountains, birdbaths, and plenty of plants.
- Set up marble garden benches for guest seating.
- Add a gilded cage of lovebirds for a finishing touch.

Music

Plan to have a harpist perform for the ceremony.

Special Touches

- Have a herald announce the beginning of the wedding ceremony.
- Have attendants blow conch shells just before the bride walks down the aisle.
- Throw sprigs of wheat on the couple, symbolizing traditional wishes for fertility. (Or update the fertility tradition with colorful streamers.)

Transportation

Bring the bride and groom to the reception in a horse-pulled Roman chariot.

Reception

Area Decor

Create your own triclinium—an ancient Roman dining room with reclining couches for dining.

- Decorate the walls with murals, frescos, and mosaics depicting Roman scenes. During the Roman empire, such scenes served as conversation pieces.
- When using food buffets, position toga-costumed actors on buffet tables to pose as live centerpieces.

Table Decor

Continue the triclinium decor with the following decorating hints:

- Place benches (or couches) with large cushions on three sides of each table (the Romans sat three to a bench). Leave the fourth side empty to allow an unobstructed view of the room. The wedding couple reclines on the couch of honor at the head of the room, resting on their left sides. Honored guests (bridal party members, family, and close friends) are seated to their right. Other guests are seated to the left.

- Cover tables with gold-lamé or purple tablecloths.
- Place large bowls of fruit on stone columns as table centerpieces. Use large pillar candles as accents.
- Use terra cotta, gold, and silver tableware.
- Decorate the outsides of serving plates with circling ivy.
- Serve wine in large pewter goblets, and have a Coup de Marriage (a two-handled wedding goblet) for the bride and groom.

Tip: The Romans ate with their fingers, which were periodically washed by slaves. But you may want to provide silverware.

Favors

The Roman bride and groom personally gave out gifts at the end of the event. You may want to follow their example. The following all make appropriate parting gifts:

- Brooches, dice and table games, vases, or small jewel boxes
- Pewter goblets, engraved with "When in Rome, Do as the Romans Do"
- Polaroid photos of guests posing in a chariot (If you don't have access to a chariot, make your own using a foam-core or wooden one-sided prop.) Or have guests pose on a fainting couch (or a pile of large pillows). Instruct them to tilt their head back, and hold a bunch of grapes above their mouth.

Tip: For a fun touch, give out bottles of Caesar's salad dressing. Print personalized labels with the wedding couple's name and wedding date.

Guest Book

Have the guests sign a large scroll. Roll the ends of the scroll with ornate, gold-painted, wooden dowels.

Entertainment

- Hire people to dress and act as Roman servants, and have them invite guests to remove their sandals and place their feet in scented oils and water just before entering the room.
- Announce each dinner guest as he or she enters the triclinium.
- Once everyone is seated, have the herald announce the beginning of the feast.

- Have toga-clad waitstaff parade trays of bite-sized food (especially important when guests eat with their hands).
- For an exciting Roman touch, have the waiters sing while serving. (This could be very pleasant, if the singers can actually sing, or very funny, if they can't. Choose the waitstaff with that in mind.)
- Arrange to have a variety of acts entertain guests between dinner courses; consider magicians, jugglers, acrobats, dancers, poets, and minstrels. Ask all entertainers to wear theme-appropriate costumes.
- Recreate an old Roman custom, and shower guests with flower petals from the ceiling during dinner.
- Play various games involving balls. The Romans played a lot of ball games, including handball, soccer, field hockey, and catch. Spray paint some balls with gold paint and throw them through hoops strung from the ceiling. Play a lawn Bocci game with gold Bocci balls. Or make up a Roman bowling game using gold-painted croquet balls and plastic Roman statues or busts.
- Conduct an archery tournament.
- Offer professional neck and foot rubs.

Menu

The Roman delicacies should be displayed and served on elaborate Roman-motif trays and platters. Create drama by pouring brandy on the food and igniting. Line trays or platters with large green leaves, and place a figurine of Priapus, the Roman god of gardens, in the center. Fill platters with an array of rich foods:

- Roasted stuffed pig, served with the head, along with warm sausages
- Variety of dishes with contrasting savory and sweet tastes: fried bread and honey, celery with leeks in honey sauce, fruit, asparagus, baked apples served in pumpkin shells, oysters, and a date and almond mixture
- Ostrich pâté or tenderloins, for an unusual modern touch
- Don't forget the Caesar salad!

Cake

- Have a baker create a cake that looks like a piece of Roman architecture, with miniature Roman figures standing around a reflecting pool.
- Top a tiered cake with a Roman statuette.
- Display sweet wine cakes or honey fruitcakes next to a traditional wedding cake.

"California Dreamin'" Beach Party Wedding

D ream of a groovy, fun-in-the-sun celebration—a perfect informal, backyard-type, summer wedding. However, you can also use this theme in the colder months to create a refreshing and sunny break during the winter doldrums. The nostalgic touches of the sixties and the fun-inspiring California-beach atmosphere are sure to bring smiles and result in a happy and memorable occasion.

Invitations

- Write, "You're Invited to a Beach Party Wedding for a groovy, fun-in-the-sun celebration" directly on an inflated beach ball. Deflate the ball before mailing.
- Create formal or informal printed invitations with the above message, and send them along with one of these novel accents:
  —Some sand and tiny seashells in a plastic bottle or bag
  —Pair of sunglasses or bottle of suntan lotion
  —Single silk daisy
  —California or surfer postcard

Guests' Dress

Ask guests to "Wear some flowers in your hair. No shoes allowed. Casual or beach wear is requested."

Wedding-Party Dress

Bride

- Choose a white go-go/sixties mini- or maxidress, and include such hip details as
  —A wreath of daisies headpiece
  —Go-go boots (or go barefoot!)

Bridal Bouquet

Have the bride carry a small bouquet of daisies or, to accent the beach theme, have her carry a seashell filled with flowers.

Groom

- Dress the groom in casual wear, such as bell-bottom pants, a vest, and moccasins (or have him go barefoot to match the bride).
- Complete the outfit with a headband and granny glasses.

Groomsmen

Dress groomsmen in tie-dyed T-shirts, bell-bottom pants or jeans, fringed vests, love beads, and peace-sign jewelry.

Bridesmaids

- Clothe bridesmaids in psychedelic-colored mini- or maxidresses, love beads, and peace-sign jewelry.
- Have each bridesmaid carry a different-colored, long-stemmed Spider Gerbera daisy.

Flower Girl

- Dress this flower child in a short, flower-print dress, love beads, and granny glasses. Paint a daisy flower on one of her cheeks with face paints.
- Have the flower girl give out a few daisies to guests as she proceeds down the aisle.

Ring Bearer

- Dress the ring bearer in sixties-style clothing similar to the groomsmen.
- Have the ring bearer carry a "Make Love, Not War!" sign in one hand and flash a peace sign with the fingers of his other hand. Punch a hole in one corner of the sign, thread a ribbon through the hole, and tie the rings onto the ribbon.

Ceremony

Wedding Site

Hold this groovy wedding at the beach. If there is no beach near you, hold the wedding by a pool or simulate an indoor beach with murals, sand on the floor, palm trees, and so on.

Decor

- Set up tent awnings to provide shade.
- Light the area with tiki torches.
- Lay out beach blankets and large, colorful beach umbrellas for the ceremony and the reception.
- Set up a lifeguard stand—this is where the bridal couple will stand to exchange wedding vows. The lifeguard stand will also provide a nice photo opportunity for guests during the reception.
- Make a wedding arch out of colorful Hula-Hoops or white-daisy garlands.

Music

Hire an acoustic-guitar musician, or play Beach Boys recordings to create that "lovin'" feeling.

Special Touches

- Hand out bottles of bubbles, personalized with the bride's and groom's names. Have the guests blow bubbles at the bride and groom after the ceremony.
- Have guests release live butterflies at the end of the ceremony. (See Supplier Resource Directory, page 162.)

Transportation

Transport the guests to the wedding—or whisk the bride and groom off to the honeymoon—in Volkswagen Beetle classic cars.

Reception

Area Decor

Hold the reception at the same location as the wedding ceremony. In addition to the decorating ideas suggested above, make buffet tables from surfboards.

Table Decor

- Cover picnic tables with tie-dyed tablecloths or beach towels.
- Make centerpieces with beach balls and other inflatable beach toys.
- Create colorful sand-pail centerpieces. Fill brightly colored pails with sand, and insert two toy shovels, one inscribed with the bride's name and the other with the groom's. You can use the colors of the pails for table-seating assignments.
- Use sunglasses for napkin rings.

Favors

- Beach towels, placed at each seat
- Love beads, sixties-style patches, and granny glasses

Tip: Have the "flower children"—flower girl and ring bearer—hand out favors during the reception.

Guest Book

Have guests autograph a large beach towel with permanent fabric markers.

Entertainment

Provide plenty of sixties fun:

- Place an actor on a tall lifeguard stand to greet guests.
- Provide life-sized "bathing beauty" cutouts for photo opportunities.
- Rent an interactive, simulated, surfing video game.
- Place temporary flower, peace sign, and smiley face tattoos on guests' cheeks, ring fingers, arms, belly buttons, and so on.
- Hold Hula-Hoop and limbo contests.
- Conduct a pool-toy relay race or underwater treasure hunt.
- Set up a volleyball net.
- Have guests design a new house for the newlyweds by building sand castles. Hold a contest for the best, funniest, most practical, most impractical, and so on.
- Build a bonfire on the beach, and roast hot dogs and marshmallows.
- Hire a deejay to spin beach tunes.
- Have a sixties rock-and-roll band perform on a floating stage in the pool.

Menu

For a fun and casual menu, serve

- Roasted hot dogs, hamburgers, and chicken
- Veggie burgers (for serious "Californians")
- Roasted ears of corn
- Chips and dip
- Fruit pizzas and fruit skewers
- Tubs of wine coolers and fruit slushies (Recruit some of the guests to help make these concoctions.)

Cake

- Serve a pineapple upside-down cake.

A "Note"-able Evening—Melodies of Love Fill the Air

T his elegant, sophisticated wedding theme captures the heart with melodic images of love. The music-note motif provides creative, distinctive touches to a traditional black-and-white theme and will certainly make a note-able impression on friends and family.

Invitations

- Write the invitation details on a piece of sheet music, directly on the staffs. Include the title "Love fills the moment, and melodies, playing images of love, fill the air." Choose one of the following mailing options:
  - —Roll the invitations into scroll shapes and tie with black satin ribbons.
  - —Lay the sheet music, unbound, inside a heavy-duty paper booklet cover. Wrap a gold nylon tassel along the folded edge.
  - —Attach a small chocolate replica of a piece of sheet music or a music note to each invitation.
  - —Send, or have each invitation hand-delivered, in a black top hat (costume or paper).

Guests' Dress

For a very formal wedding, specify "Black Tie" on the invitation. For a semiformal evening, ask guests to wear black-and-white clothing.

Wedding-Party Dress

Bride

- Dress in a romantic, sophisticated, floor-length bridal gown. Choose a bridal shop gown or design your own:
  - —Figure-hugging, satin, sleeveless column dress, with the shoulders, chest, and arms covered by sheer silk tulle

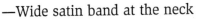

—Wide satin band at the neck

—Satin, bell-shaped cuffs at the wrists, covering the hands up to the knuckles

—Satin buttons on the back of the dress to close the tulle bodice

• Complete the look with a glorious, billowing, layered veil. Gather the veil at the top of the head to build height, and then add plenty of layers to fall at shoulder length, with one sheer layer cascading all the way to the floor.

Bridal Bouquet

Make a "note"-able statement with any one of the following bridal bouquets:

• Carry a large bouquet of calla lilies.

• Make a holding cone out of sheet music for the bouquet.

• Decorate the outside edges of a nosegay bouquet with a sheet-music doily.

Groom

• Clothe the groom in the most formal full-evening dress:

—Black tailcoat

—White wing-collar piqué shirt

—White piqué vest and bow

• Complete the look with a top hat, a cane, and a pair of black patent leather shoes.

Groomsmen

To follow the rules of etiquette for very formal occasions, dress the groomsmen identically to the groom.

Bridesmaids

• Select straight, floor-length, shoulderless, black, satin gowns, and accent with these striking details:

—Long, white, satin gloves

—Wide and very long black satin ribbon wrapped around the neck (Tie the bow at the nape of the neck, and let the long ribbon tails stream down the back of the dress. Style bridesmaids' hair up, or wear short, to reveal the bows.)

—Small, black, beaded purses

Flower Girl

• Dress the flower girl in one of the following:
   —Frilly white dress
   —Charming white-with-black-polka-dots dress
   —Dress with a music-note motif
• Trim the dress with a wide black ribbon tied around the waist and tied into a large bow in the back.
• Include white, lace-trimmed anklet socks and black patent leather shoes.
• Add a white straw hat and short white gloves.
• Give the flower girl a small black hatbox filled with rose petals to drop along the way.

Ring Bearer

• Dress the ring bearer identically to the groom and groomsmen (just omit the cane).
• Place the rings inside a top hat, and have the ring bearer carry the hat down the aisle.

Ceremony

Wedding Site

Hold a candlelight service in a concert hall or place of worship.

Decor

• Illuminate the aisle and room with candlelight. In addition, give each guest a candle to hold, and have guests light each other's candles. Start by lighting the candles of two guests seated on each side of the front row. Tell these guests to light the candle of the person next to them, and so on, until all the candles in the room are lit.
• Adorn the site with white flowers and white pew bows.
• Decorate wedding programs with a sheet-music design.

Music

Play recorded music that captures the essence of love:

—Bizet: Intermezzo from *Carmen,* Act III

—Bach: Minuet from *Anna Magdelena*

—Rimsky-Korsakov: *Scheherezade*

—Mozart: Piano Concerto no. 21

Special Touches

Shoot a confetti cannon, containing black-and-white confetti, over the couple as they share their first kiss as husband and wife.

Transportation

Whisk the bride and groom off to the reception in a black stretch limousine packed with champagne and romantic music.

Reception

Area Decor

Hold the reception in an elegant hotel or event site ballroom, and decorate the site with musical splendor:

• Lay down a black-and-white checkerboard dance floor.

• Place white flower arrangements on black-lacquered pillars.

• Frame the stage with large music notes.

• Make a photo gallery display with family members' wedding photos, including Mom and Dad, Grandma and Grandpa, Sister and Brother-in-Law, and so on. Below each photo, list the name of a favorite song, or one that is reminiscent of the couple.

• Shine gobo lights (light-projected images) onto the walls, choosing music notes and dancing-bride-and-groom-silhouette designs.

• Display music-note-shaped ice sculptures around the room.

Table Decor

• Cover tables with floor-length, black tablecloths, and accent with crisp white napkins.

• Use musical-instrument Christmas tree ornaments as napkin holders.

• Tie black sash bows around white chair covers.

- Reverse the color scheme of the above table design with white table-cloths, black napkins, and white sash bows around black chair covers. Alternate the two color schemes throughout the room.
- Attach miniature music boxes to napkin rings or place cards.
- Place single red roses across each napkin.
- Place music stands with dinner menus next to the tables.
- Make a grand statement with baby-grand-piano tables. To make the table tops, cut out a piece of plywood into the shape of the top of a baby grand piano. Secure the "piano" table tops to the banquet tables with screws. Paint the wood with black lacquer paint, and paint the black-and-white keyboard design at the "keyboard" end of the tables (or make a keyboard design with foam core pieces). Do not cover these tables with a tablecloth, but do hang black skirting around the edges of the tables to create a 3-D effect. Set a large candelabra and a bust of Beethoven on each table, and place a music stand with sheet music on the floor nearby. Each "piano table" seats about eight people; make enough tables for all your guests, or only for the wedding party.
- Try one of these creative centerpiece ideas:
  —Short music stands holding folders of classical sheet music (Use a different piece of music for each table, and assign seating according to the sheet music title.)
  —Silver candelabra stands with tall tapered candles
  —White floral arrangements with actual musical instruments: violins, French horns, and clarinets
  —Music notes or ballroom dancer silhouettes made from black-gloss-covered foam core
  —A pair of stuffed white men's tuxedo gloves reaching from inside a top hat (Cover the opening of the hat with decorative metallic grass. Form the glove "hands" to stretch upward. Place a piece of sheet music or a black music note in the hands.)

Favors

- Cassette tapes of romantic songs with the bride's and groom's names and wedding date printed on the covers
- Small boxes of chocolates wrapped in sheet music or music-note wrapping paper
- Silver or gold music-note tie tacks and charm bracelets

Guest Book

Have guests sign a folder of sheet music.

Entertainment

Provide musical entertainment to complete this spectacular wedding celebration:

- Place a circular riser, holding an actual grand piano, in the center of the room. Hire a pianist to play classical tunes during dinner.
- Hire a jazz band, big band, or orchestra for dancing.
- Contact a talent agency for a song-and-dance review.
- Entertain guests with strolling violinists during dinner.
- Produce a slide show of the bride and groom, from childhood to courtship, choreographed to music. Try such songs as "You've Got the Cutest Little Baby Face," "First Love," "Sentimental Journey," and so on. Hire an actor to dress in an orchestra conductor's "maestro" costume and guide the guests through the musical slide show.
- Have the maestro introduce the bride and groom for their first dance.
- Have a song written especially for the couple, set to a popular tune. Print the song on decorative cards, and give one to each guest. Have the maestro lead the group in singing the song to the happy couple.
- Organize the guests to put on a fun skit for the wedding couple: Ask each guest to bring a musical instrument they do *not* play, or provide fun instruments yourself: kazoos, drums made from Kentucky Fried Chicken buckets and chopsticks, bells, tambourines, and so on. Divide the guests into groups, and randomly distribute the musical instruments. Instruct each group to step to the side, decide on a song, rehearse, if they like, and then return and perform for the wedding couple. This is a fun, casual, and hilarious skit.
- Try this fun mixer idea: Write the name of a romantic song on one batch of cards, another song name on another batch of cards, and so on, depending on the size of the wedding and the desired size of the groups. Hand out the cards to the guests, and tell them to find other guests with the same song title. After all groups assemble, ask them to sing their song to the couple. *Hint:* Do not tell the groups beforehand that they will be singing the song.
- Or do a slight variation of the above mixer activity: Hand out cards with romantic song titles as you did above. Place matching cards on the tables, and instruct guests to sit at the table with the sign matching

their card. After the guests have been seated, ask them to sing their song, one table at a time.

- Write various love song titles on cards and decorate the cards with ribbons. Give each guest a card and instruct them to sing out a line of the song on their card each time they want the wedding couple to kiss. Use popular, easily recognizable song titles, or write out a line that contains the song's title, highlighted.

Menu

Serve an elegant, seated dinner. Consider the following:

- Silver-tray hors d'oeuvres service
- Tossed greens and mushroom salad served with lemon vinaigrette dressing
- Salmon steak, rice pilaf, and asparagus with hollandaise sauce
- White chocolate mousse in a chocolate piano-shaped mold

Cake

Choose a wedding cake to enhance the musical theme:

- Place a music box on top of the cake.
- Have your baker design a cake in the shape of a baby grand piano.
- Order an elaborate, tiered cake, and top it with a miniature baby grand piano figurine. Write titles of romantic songs on the outside of each tier.

Love in Any Language—A Valentine Wedding

I talians cry, "*amoré;*" the French whisper, "*amour;*" Germans declare, "*liebe;*" and the Spanish profess, "*amor.*" Love, in any language, fills the hearts of the Valentine wedding couple. Celebrate this special holiday wedding with international flair. Don't reserve this theme just for Valentine's Day, either; the international flavor and romantic statements make this theme a "love"-ly statement any day of the year.

Invitations

Turn any wedding day into Valentine's Day with fanciful invitations:

- Place a traditional engraved invitation inside an empty chocolate candy heart box decorated with plenty of lace, flowers, and ribbon.
- Enclose a single piece of heart-shaped candy, a box of candy conversation hearts, or a toy arrow with each invitation.
- Print invitation details on a valentine.
- Arrange to have the invitations sent and postmarked from romantic-sounding locations: Loveland, Colorado; Kissimee, Florida; Love, Mississippi; Romance, Arkansas; or Eros, Louisiana.
- Attach a separate note asking guests to bring a valentine to exchange at the wedding reception.

Guests' Dress

Invite guests to come dressed in traditional "romantic" wedding attire.

Wedding-Party Dress

Bride

- Create one of the following sweetheart gowns:
  - —Figure-hugging, long-sleeved bodice
  - —V-shaped neckline that lies just below the shoulders
  - —Satin skirt that flows over billowing clouds of tulle skirting and puffy crinoline underskirting (Showcase the delicate tulle skirting with a split draping cut in the front of the satin skirt.)

  or

  - —Tightly fitting, satin, heart-shaped sleeveless bodice
  - —Transparent silk tulle covering the chest, shoulders, and arms
  - —Satin-accented trim for the neckline and sleeves
  - —Satin buttons on the back of the dress to close the bodice
  - —Multilayered, billowing, three-quarter-length silk tulle skirt gathered at the waist
- Attach a full, shoulder-length bridal veil to a pearl headband worn across the forehead.
- Wear delicate satin ballet slippers.
- Accessorize with a romantic heart locket.

Bridal Bouquet

Make a bouquet out of red sweetheart roses and a lace nosegay. Attach a few small hearts to white satin ribbon streamers.

Groom

- Dress the groom in a romantic outfit of a gray classic stroller with striped trousers, a pearl-gray vest, and a white pleated formal shirt.
- Complete the look with a four-in-hand tie, white gloves, and a gray Homburg (a felt hat with a soft, dented crown).
- Pin on a red sweetheart rose boutonniere.

Groomsmen

Dress groomsmen identically to the groom, but give them white rose boutonnieres instead of red.

Bridesmaids

- Choose a red, satin, ballerina-length dress with a wide, full skirt lying over a stiff white crinoline underskirt. A portrait neckline, one that rests just above the shoulders and gathers to a point in the low center bust line, is a flattering design.
- Add short white gloves and pillbox hats with short puffy veils.
- Have bridesmaids carry heart-shaped purses.

Flower Girl

- Dress the flower girl in a white crinoline dress with red heart designs.
- Give the flower girl a white wicker basket filled with white paper doily hearts to drop along the bride's path.

Ring Bearer

- Dress the ring bearer in red satin short pants and jacket.
- Tie the wedding rings onto an elaborately decorated (empty) heart-shaped chocolate candy box.

Tip: In addition to the flower girl and the ring bearer, dress a small child as Cupid to start the wedding procession.

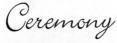

Ceremony

Wedding Site

Hold the ceremony in a house of worship or alternative wedding site.

Decor

Decorate the area with romantic splendor:

- Make two floral arrangements in the shape of the bride's first initial and the groom's first initial. Hang the two initials on the site's outside doors.
- Decorate the site with white and red flowers.
- For the wedding vow exchange, place tall white columns holding cherub urns and red flowers on each side of the wedding party.

- Unroll a white runner down the aisle for the bridal party procession.
- During the winter, in colder climate areas, make a love offering to the birds. Press birdseed into heart shapes on top of the snow.
- Write the word "love" in several different languages on the wedding program.

Music

Hire a harpist to play during the ceremony.

Special Touches

- Release white doves as the bride and groom exchange their first kiss. (Be sure to use a professional animal trainer to release and recover the doves to ensure the safety of the animals and the wedding audience.)
- Float origami doves over the guests—hang them from a balcony or the ceiling.
- Give the guests small, heart-shaped boxes filled with rice or pink-and-white heart-shaped confetti to throw on the couple after the ceremony. If showering the couple outdoors, substitute the rice with birdseed; rice is harmful for birds to eat.

Transportation

Whisk the bride and groom off to the reception in a horse-drawn carriage.

Reception

Area Decor

- Bring the red-and-white floral arrangements from the wedding ceremony to the reception site.
- Place swans in a water fountain or reflecting pond, and sprinkle the water with red rose petals.
- Hang framed posters of romantic international destinations: the Eiffel Tower in Paris, castles in Germany, fountains in Rome, whitewashed buildings and brilliant-blue waters of the Greek Islands, and so on.
- Print the word "love," written in different languages, on decorative hearts, and place them on corresponding international buffet tables.

Table Decor

- Cover tables with floor-length red tablecloths and white satin or lace table toppers.
- Tie red roses to white linen napkins with red satin ribbons, and set at each place setting.
- Rent gold cane chairs.
- Use gold urns, angels, or Cupid statues (filled or decorated with white carnations and red sweetheart roses) for centerpieces.
- Set out heart-shaped topiary trees as centerpieces.
- Place heart-shaped menu cards at each place setting.
- Insert menu cards into elaborate gold-colored frames.

Favors

- Randomly placed valentines (that guests have brought) at each place setting (Plan to have extras, for those who forget to bring a valentine.)
- Decorative cards printed with this explanation for the Valentine tradition: "One early belief regarding the origin of St. Valentine's Day is rooted in the Roman Festival of Lupercalia, celebrating the coming of spring. Roman maidens wrote their names on slips of paper and collected the slips in an urn. Each available man drew a name from the urn, and he then courted the chosen girl for the next year, often writing her love notes during this time—thus the Valentine."
- Small gift boxes with chocolate candy, decorated with the bride's and groom's initials, tied with pretty bows, and attached to small cards reading, "Be my Valentine." (On the back of the cards, print table numbers. As the guests enter the reception area, give each guest a box. It serves as a sweet memento and a unique table assignment card.)
- Cards imprinted with the word "love" written in different languages (For example, print *amoré, amour,* or *liebe.* Ask the guests to sit at the table with the sign matching their card.)

Guest Book

Have guests write their names and wedding wishes for the bride and groom on red, white, and pink hearts (or heart-shaped doilies or the backs of children's Valentines). Collect the hearts in an empty heart-shaped candy box.

Entertainment

Entertain guests with international expressions of love through the universal language of music and fun:

- Arrange for vocal performances of love songs in various languages.
- Have a woodwind ensemble and harpist play during the reception.
- Have a violinist stroll from table to table during dinner.
- Set up a Cupid's arrow target shooting range. Attach a large red paper heart in the center of the target.

Menu

Buffets work well for this theme. Set up buffet tables with international offerings, representing Asian, Mexican, Italian, French, and other cuisines. The following are also nice touches:

- Heart-shaped dinner rolls
- Flambé station for Cherries Jubilee, Bananas Flambé, and so on

Cake

- Order one large heart-shaped cake or a tier cake made with heart-shaped cakes.
- Place a small nosegay of red sweetheart roses on top of the cake.
- Make an old-fashioned Red Velvet Cake—a red-colored cocoa cake.
- Next to the cake, place decorative heart-shaped candy boxes. Open them, and prop them up for display.

"Once Upon a Time" Wedding Ball

W hat can be more romantic than the age-old story of Cinderella meeting her Prince Charming? The origin and time period of Cinderella, as of any folktale told through the ages in many different cultures, is unknown. Many variations of the story of the lost slipper or sandal have been found in manuscripts of ancient India, Egypt, and Greece, and on the lips of storytellers in Zulu huts, Indian hogans, and Samoan villages. For us, the most familiar adaptation is probably the version found in *Grimms' Popular Stories* (or *Grimms' Fairy Tales*, as they are known), first translated into English in 1823. The most visual adaptations, by far, are the 1950 Disney cartoon and 1964 film version of Rogers and Hammerstein's musical, both of which chose the Renaissance era as their setting. This wedding theme also uses the Renaissance era, but you can choose any era—the twenties (1920s), present day, or even space-age future. The romance of a fairy tale, including your own, is timeless.

Invitations

Give your invitations a fairy-tale look:

- Format the invitations to look and read like small storybooks. Use Old English script, and enclose a gold-tassel bookmark with each "book."

- Write: Once upon a time there was a young girl, named [bride's name]. One day her fairy godmother appeared and granted [bride's name] a magic wish. [bride's name] wished to "live happily ever after" with her Prince Charming, [groom's name]. You're invited to take part in this magical union at their Fairy-Tale Wedding Ball on [wedding date].

Guests' Dress

Include a note with the invitation saying, "Ladies, you are invited to wear your ball gowns, and men, your formal attire." Traditional wedding attire is also appropriate for this theme. If you have added a particular era to your theme, such as "futuristic space-age" or "Victorian," include this information also. For example: "Dress in space-age ballroom wear."

Wedding-Party Dress

Bride

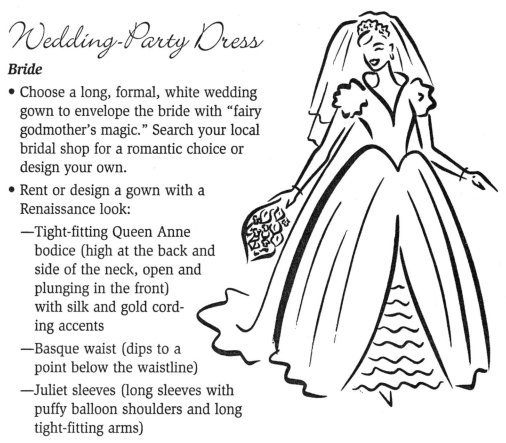

- Choose a long, formal, white wedding gown to envelope the bride with "fairy godmother's magic." Search your local bridal shop for a romantic choice or design your own.

- Rent or design a gown with a Renaissance look:

  —Tight-fitting Queen Anne bodice (high at the back and side of the neck, open and plunging in the front) with silk and gold cording accents

  —Basque waist (dips to a point below the waistline)

  —Juliet sleeves (long sleeves with puffy balloon shoulders and long tight-fitting arms)

  —Wide, flowing skirt with padded hips, slit in the front to show the underskirting

- Add a cathedral train from the shoulders.

- Choose a heavy brocade material in gold or white.

- Add a sparkling tiara, holding layers of veiling.

- Select a pair of Cinderella-like "glass slippers." Choose white satin low-heeled pumps, dress flats, or ballet-like slippers decorated with iridescent pearls, sequins, or beads. Bridal salons and department stores sometimes carry a clear plastic pump-style shoe, especially around the holidays. However, these shoes will most likely be too uncomfortable to wear for any long stretches of time. You may want to buy a pair to use for the "glass slipper fit" stunt or as a decorative prop.

Bridal Bouquet

Design a cascading arrangement of gold roses, gardenias, and lilies, accented with a hint of pearls and tiny sparkling faux jewels.

Groom

- Costume the groom as a prince:
  - —Velvet doublet (a close-fitting and waisted jacket) covering a shirt with ballooning oversleeves
  - —Puffed-out breeches and hose (If the groom prefers a more-modern adaptation, substitute tight-fitting slacks for the breeches and hose.)
  - —Soft, leather, ballet-type or velvet, above-the-ankle-and-pointed-toe shoes
- Add a ruff (a stiff, ruffled, circular collar), a prince's crown, and a velvet cape.

Groomsmen

Dress groomsmen similarly to the groom, but substitute velvet, plumed hats for the prince's crown.

Bridesmaids

- Dress bridesmaids in straight gowns with high waistlines that fit closely across the bust and then flow loosely to the ground.
- Choose gold-colored, light satin brocade material for warmer months and velvet for colder months.
- Add ornate Renaissance-style hats like those worn by the female guests in the 1964 Cinderella film. The most popular and recognizable style is the henin (a tall, cone-like hat with a veil draping from its point). There are many variations to the hat styles of this era; some of the padded rolls and double-point versions are amusing and almost absurd.
- For a more subtle statement, braid the bridesmaids' hair with flowers, or place their coiffures in elaborate hair nets. Basically, choose a head-piece style that best fits with the rest of the theme details.
- Have bridesmaids carry small bouquets of lilies or wildflowers.

Flower Girl

- Costume the flower girl as Cinderella before she went to the ball:
  - —Peasant-style dress with a white, square-neck chemise, laced bodice, and a tattered-edge skirt
  - —Handkerchief-scarf head covering
- Have the flower girl carry a wood-looking pail (make sure it is light) filled with rose petals to scatter along the bridal path.

Ring Bearer

- Dress the ring bearer in a costume similar to the groom's.
- Have the ring bearer carry the rings in a glass-looking Cinderella slipper placed upon a red velvet pillow adorned with gold braiding and tassels.

Wedding Site

Hold the wedding ceremony in a house of worship or in an elegant hotel or ballroom.

Decor

- Use tall, ornate candelabra stands to frame the ceremony space.
- Hang flower garlands on the outside of the pews or other seating.
- Roll a red carpet down the center aisle.
- Have the groomsmen form an arch of shiny swords for the wedding procession.
- Decorate the trees outside the site with long, flowing ribbons.

Music

- Have a Renaissance-clad musician announce the beginning of the wedding procession with a clarion (a long, straight medieval trumpet). Contact your local Renaissance Festival for a resource, or hire someone who plays a traditional trumpet or bugle.
- During the service, have a hammer-dulcimer and/or harpist play romantic tunes.
- If the worship site has bells, ring them before and after the service.

Special Touches

- Have a costumed "Fairy Godmother" actress or the bride's mother (dressed in regular wedding attire) lightly tap the bride on the head with a magic wand to start the exchange of wedding vows.
- When the bride and groom kiss after exchanging vows, release doves. Hire a professional animal trainer to coordinate this display for the animals' and guests' safety.
- Have the Prince (groom) try to fit the bride with Cinderella's glass slipper as part of the marriage ceremony (or as a reception activity).

- Give guests magic wands adorned with small plastic bottles of iridescent confetti. Have guests remove the lids and wave the magic wands at the wedding couple, showering them with glittering magic dust.

Transportation

Whisk the bride and groom away to the reception, and later to their honeymoon, in a Pumpkin Carriage, of course.

Reception

Area Decor

Let the elegant ambiance of a hotel ballroom, complete with high ceilings and elaborate chandeliers, be the scene of a palace ballroom. In addition:

- Have a set designer build a castle-wall-and-turret entrance.
- Hang a backdrop with a painting of a winding staircase. At the top of the staircase, paint a large grandfather clock, its hands approaching midnight. (Or place real grandfather clocks in the ballroom, with all the hands stopped at midnight.)
- Place life-sized wire sculptures wrapped with sparkling lights, available commercially, around the room. Request, or have a set designer create, a pumpkin coach, a fairy godmother, or a giant glass slipper.
- Cover the dance floor with a layer of white, clear, and opalescent balloons. If you use gold as part of the area decor, add a few gold balloons.

Table Decor

- Canopy the head table, and decorate it with floral garlands.
- Hang colorful flag banners (with coat-of-arms or Renaissance-like markings) from the ceiling above the head table.
- Place candelabra stands behind the bride and groom.
- Cover all chairs with royal colors: purple, emerald green, or gold.
- Cover guest tables with floor-length, white tablecloths and gathered overlays.
- For centerpieces, choose one of the following designs or alternate more than one:
  —Velvet pillows with gold braiding and tassels, each holding a Cinderella slipper (Fill the slippers with roses, and have some rose petals spill onto the pillows.)

—Gold-painted pumpkins filled with fresh flowers (Cut the bottom of the pumpkin to lie flat, leaving enough so the pumpkin remains watertight.)

- Place centerpieces on round mirrors, lay a fairy godmother star wand next to each, and surround with votive candles.
- Set out small, clear, plastic slippers filled with mints at each place setting. (These also make fun favors.)

Favors

- Boxes of chocolates that look like storybooks, with the title "Once Upon a Time" inscribed on each one
- Crystal glass slippers
- Shiny, gold-painted miniature pumpkins (These make nice place-setting favors and fun place cards.)

Guest Book

Have guests write their names with a large feather quill pen on the pages of an oversized fairy-tale book.

Entertainment

- Hire a string quartet or a harpist to play as guests enter the room.
- Hire an actress to dress as the fairy godmother to greet guests. She can wave a magic wand, showering guests with magic dust (glitter or confetti).
- Have the waitstaff dress like royal servants and offer guests champagne served from silver trays.
- Have the costumed servers bring the food in a festive procession while majestic music plays in the background.
- Have an orchestra play after dinner, so guests can waltz away the evening.
- Search for Prince Charming's princess. Seat each available maiden on a throne or chair, one at time. Have Prince Charming (the groom) try to slip a Cinderella slipper onto each lady's foot, ending with his princess, the bride. *Hint:* Stuff the shoe with tissue, removing it for the bride, to ensure that the slipper only fits the bride.
- Hold a Cinderella Shoe Hunt. Have all guests pile their shoes in the middle of the dance floor, then hide a Cinderella slipper in the middle of the pile. At the emcee's cue, instruct guests to find their own shoes. Award a prize to the first person who finds his or her own shoes, plus a prize to the person who finds the Cinderella slipper.

Menu

For a sit-down dinner:

- Cornish hen, rice, seasonal vegetable, soup, and salad
- Different wines with each course
- Chocolate slippers filled with mousse or berries

For a buffet dinner:

- Bountiful and beautiful display of fruit and cheese around an ice sculpture of—what else—a glass slipper!
- Roast leg of lamb, ham, and turkey
- Variety of salads and potato and rice dishes
- Dessert buffet
- Vanilla ice cream swirled with honey and sunflower seeds

Cake

- Choose a traditional tiered cake or ask a baker to make a fairy-tale creation:

    —Five-foot-high tiered structure

    —Castle-shaped cake
- Add a groom's cake designed as an open storybook with the title "Once Upon a Time."

Wedding South of the Border

exican cuisine and southwestern decor are very popular, especially for summer celebrations. So, why not create some "south of the border" fun and ambiance for your wedding ceremony and reception? This wedding theme is not meant to be an authentic representation of Mexican weddings, but rather, is created to celebrate the festive spirit of Mexico and to relish Mexican cultural influences.

Invitations

Invite guests to celebrate this wedding with some "south of the border" fun:

- Attach each wedding invitation to a large, colorful paper flower.
- Tie a dried chili pepper, tiny sombrero, or miniature Mexican flag to each invitation.
- Write invitation details on flour tortillas or Mexico travel brochures.
- For a novelty touch, send a card along with each invitation, instructing guests to call the enclosed telephone number. Set up a voice-mail message with Mexican background music, and record the invitation in Spanish. Offer an English translation at the end of the tape.

Guests' Dress

For a more formal wedding, encourage guests to dress in traditional wedding attire. In this case, you don't have to print any special instructions on the invitations. For a more casual wedding, you could print "South of the Border Wear Suggested" on the invitation. Be sure your suggestion is diplomatic and courteous to the Mexican culture.

Wedding-Party Dress

Bride

- Choose a traditional white gown with a wide scoop neck and traditional veil, adding some southwestern accents:

—Native American/Mexican-design wide-beaded necklace

—Pair of white cowboy boots

Bridal Bouquet

Choose one of these charming bridal bouquet designs:

- Lightweight bouquet of white flowers, carried with a rosary and a small white Bible
- Bouquet of wildflowers, such as daisies, saffron, black-eyed Susans, and hollyhocks (Wrap a string of turquoise-like beads around the stems.)

Groom

Give the groom that south-of-the-border look with a sombrero, short embroidered jacket, bolero tie, and full-length pants.

Groomsmen

Dress groomsmen similarly to the groom.

Bridesmaids

- Choose off-the-shoulder ruffle blouses and full, striped Mexican-design skirts.
- Have bridesmaids carry bouquets of brightly colored paper flowers.

Flower Girl

- Dress the flower girl similarly to the bridesmaids.
- Give the flower girl tissue-paper flowers to toss along the bridal path.

Ring Bearer

- Dress the ring bearer in a mariachi costume.
- Have the ring bearer carry the rings inside a sombrero.

Ceremony

Wedding Site

Hold the wedding in a hacienda-style house, Spanish mission, Mexican restaurant, or adobe-style building.

Decor

Let the authentic surroundings of the wedding site envelope guests in south-of-the-border splendor. If you like, create your own atmosphere using some of the suggestions listed under Reception/Area Decor.

Music

Provide organ music and a mariachi band for the wedding. Have the mariachi band play as guests enter and leave the building.

Special Touches

- Give each guest a miniature sombrero filled with rice to throw at the newly married couple. If showering the couple outdoors, substitute the rice with birdseed; rice is harmful for the birds to eat.
- For Catholic weddings, consider adding a lasso to the service. The priest places a lasso (a large rosary) around the couple to symbolize the union of the family with God.

Transportation

For some fun, have the bride and groom ride donkeys to the ceremony. The donkeys will be great for reception entertainment and photo opportunities. (Have an animal trainer handle the donkeys, to avoid any mishaps.)

Reception

Area Decor

- Take advantage of the authentic surroundings of the wedding site, or create a south-of-the-border atmosphere with Mexican cantina set designs. Include these details:
  - —Adobe walls
  - —Serapes, sombreros, maracas, and piñatas (Lay serapes across the tablecloths as decorations.)
  - —Cacti and large colorful paper flowers
  - —Strings of colorful lights and Mexican-flag streamers
  - —Earthenware bowls on the buffet
  - —Luminarias lining the entrance walkway and/or general reception area
  - —Burro flower carts and vendor carts holding large, colorful paper flowers and tequila lollipops
  - —Bar area with tent awnings and hanging lights
- Set up a Tijuana gift shop to display wedding gifts.

Table Decor

- Choose four or five hot salsa colors for tablecloths and napkins.
- Set out piñatas, cacti, sombreros, and maracas as centerpieces.
- Accent the centerpieces with pillar candles placed in clay flowerpot saucers.
- Wrap napkins with chili-pepper napkin rings.
- Make creative napkin rings by gluing small boxes of Mexican jumping beans to raffia bows.
- Wrap napkins with natural or turquoise-colored raffia bows.
- Display table assignment place cards on an earthenware or basket-weave tray, lined with loose, uncooked Indian corn kernels.

Favors

- Place-seating favors: Write the bride's and groom's names on tiny clay flower pots. Fill the pots with moss. Wrap an ink pen with florist's tape, leaving the writing end exposed. Attach leaf accents and a flower bloom at the end of the pen. Stick one pen "posy" into each flower pot.
- Tiny sombreros filled with birdseed (See Special Touches.)

- Decorative theme-shaped, iced sugar cookies (See Cake.)
- Mexican-jumping-bean napkin rings (See Table Decor.)
- Polaroid photos taken near the "Just Married—South of the Border" set (See Entertainment.)

Guest Book

Have guests sign a large travel poster depicting deep blue water and white sandy beaches of a Mexican resort.

Entertainment

- Have greeters dressed in native Mexican costumes welcome guests at the door.
- Entertain guests with a mariachi band.
- Set up a photo area with a traditionally decorated "Just Married" automobile—covered with tissue flowers, tin cans, dangling shoes, and a sign reading "Just Married—South of the Border!" Guests can pose with the bride and groom on or in the car for instant Polaroid shots. An open convertible works great for this.
- Play a "Yes or No" bean mixer game. The object of this game is to encourage mingling. Give ten uncooked beans to each player. Each time a guest answers yes or no to a question, he or she must give one bean to the player posing the question. Tell the guests to play until the deejay or emcee announces the end of the game and instructs the players to count their beans. Award a prize to the player with the most beans.
- Demonstrate how piñatas are made.
- Break a wedding-cake-shaped piñata.
- Hire a group of dancers dressed in Mexican costumes to put on a show.
- Give salsa dance lessons.
- Conduct a Mexican hat dance.
- Dispense large paper flowers and tequila lollipops from flower and vendor carts. (See Area Decor.)

Menu

The foods for this wedding should be hot and spicy. Provide some mild alternatives for guests with special diets or mild tastes.
- Burritos, enchiladas, and tacos
- Stuffed jalapeño peppers, quesadillas, spicy black beans

- Tortilla chips and nachos with salsa and guacamole
- Fajita bar
- Chocolate- and caramel-dipped tortilla chips
- Sopaipillas served from vendor carts (Sopaipillas are sweetened, fried triangle dough pockets. Traditionally, the eater bites off one end of the pocket and fills it with honey.)
- Margaritas served from a flowing fountain or from a margarita bar

Cake

- Create a cake to look like an adobe house or a sombrero.
- Choose a traditional tiered cake, but accent it with brightly colored fresh flowers.
- Complete the cake table with the following additions:
  —Iced sugar cookies (shaped as cacti, sombreros, donkeys, and wedding cakes) wrapped in cellophane corsage bags and tied with ribbons
  —Chocolate coffee cups filled with flaming liqueur

A Victorian Wedding Tea

P robably the most popular of theme weddings, a Victorian celebration is a beautiful expression of idealized romance. Unlike many royals, Queen Victoria married for love and made a conscientious effort to plan a wedding that was neither indulgent nor excessive. She wore a white satin gown with orange-blossom trim. This was considered very plain compared to the elaborate silver threads, jewel trims, crowns, and fur-lined robes of other royals. Actually, although Victoria's gown appeared simple for the times, it was extraordinarily valuable—several hundred women worked on the antique-lace gown. Queen Victoria's tiered cake design is still the traditional design today, although her cake was rumored to weigh 300 pounds. Add some Victorian elegance to your wedding to create a day as enchanting as the love that ties two hearts together.

Invitations

Design the invitation with Victorian grace and beauty:
- Send formal invitations, printed with an Old English font.
- Have a calligrapher write wedding details on Victorian stationery.
- Deliver each invitation with a single rose.
- Enclose a Victorian fan or a tea cup and saucer with each invitation.
- Send a love poem penned on delicate stationery with formal invitations. Or, have a poet create invitation verse in the form of a love poem. Ask a printer to duplicate the handwritten poem on invitation-card stock or on personal stationery. (Ask a talented friend for help or contact a local writer's club or association.)

Guests' Dress

Suggest traditional formal wear (no invitation notation needed). If you like, include "Victorian Costumes, Optional" on the invitation.

Wedding-Party Dress

Bride

The Victorian era produced a great variety of styles. The low décolletage and wide hoop skirts (like those depicted in the movie *Gone with the Wind*) were replaced by high necklines and long tight skirts (so tight around the knees, they made walking difficult). Bustles came into popularity, left, then came back for a short time. Ladies' hats ranged from soft linen caps and bonnets to straw hats and turbans. Large, decorated hats were very popular during the middle of the century, and small, stylish hats were often decorated with birds' nests. No matter what the style, an enormous amount of attention was given to details. Layers of lace, ruffles, embroidery, velvet, bows, fabric flowers, fringe, tassels, and other decorative accents were incorporated into dress designs. Many of the original dresses, dress pieces, accessories, and patterns can still be easily found in vintage dress shops, antique shops, and even over the Internet. Victorian designs are also available in most bridal shops. Select a design to fit your personal style. Following are some popular Victorian choices:

- Choose a white or ecru silk or satin gown. Blue was also a popular color with Victorian brides.

- Look for a high-necked bodice with a V-shaped ruffle insert starting at the shoulders and ending at the bust line. The chemisette or fill-in was often sheer and flesh-colored.

- Choose either a fitted bodice with a distinctive Basque (point) waist, or one with a blouson blouse bodice drawn tightly at the waist with a wide sash bow.

- Include long lines of delicate buttons to fasten the back of the bodice.

- Consider adding a decorative, high collar and a waist-length cape or a fitted jacket with a flair extending from the waist to just above the hips.

- Select either a long, tailored, fitted skirt or a long, slim, loose-flowing skirt.

- Consider adding a bustle to expand the back of the skirt.

- Finish the gown with sleeves that are either wide, puffy, and frilly or narrow and lacy. (Styles varied through this period, but the leg-o'-mutton sleeve is probably the most recognizable. This sleeve is full, puffy, and rounded at the shoulder, then abruptly straight and fitted below the elbow.)
- Choose a band of orange blossoms and a floor-length veil for the bride's headpiece. Another popular choice is a large hat decorated with flowers (sometimes feathers) and veiling. Secure it with an ornate hat pin.
- Add some dainty and feminine details to the wedding ensemble:
  —Cameo brooch at the neck
  —Gloves (or Victorian-style lace mittens), lace hankie, small, beaded purse, or parasol
  —Boot-like shoes, called high shoes (actually a Victorian outdoor shoe): above the ankle boots, secured by laces or several buttons, with pointed or square toes
  —Silk, satin, or velvet small-heeled pump (with or without a strap) decorated with fancy bows, trim, lace, and so on, to resemble Victorian formal footwear

Tip: Extend the Victorian theme to the wedding ring. According to custom, the wedding band consisted of a row of gems that "spelled out" a meaningful word. For example, Regard rings were very popular. To create a Regard ring, choose a "r"uby, an "e"merald, a "g"arnet, an "a"methyst, another "r"uby, and a "d"iamond.

Bridal Bouquet

- Copy a popular Victorian design—the Tussy Mussie. This is a bouquet of concentric circles of different flowers placed in a tight, round design. (As with the ring, the flower's names can spell out a special word or the groom's name—"m"um, "i"ris, a leaf of "k"ale, and a small "e"vergreen twig to spell "Mike.")
- Place cut flowers into an antique silver, ivory, or gold posy holder. Choose your favorite flowers, a simple springtime sprig of lilacs, a small bouquet of tulips, or a small bunch of roses. Depending on the design of the antique posy holder, you may have to add a small modern-day florist's tube to keep the flowers fresh.

Groom

Dress the groom in very formal full-dress wear (black tailcoat, white waistcoat, trousers, shirt, tie, and top hat). Today, men's formal wear is similar to men's early-Victorian fashion. Later, frock coats with double-breasted waistcoats, striped trousers, high-collar shirts with ties, patent leather button boots, gloves, and top hats became popular. Either style would make an excellent choice for today's Victorian groom. Instead of a floral boutonniere, pin a white ribbon decoration onto the groom's lapel.

Groomsmen

Dress groomsmen similarly to the groom.

Bridesmaids

- Apply a nineteenth-century custom and design bridesmaids' gowns that are different than the bride's (and in pastel colors). For example, dress two bridesmaids in light blue dresses and two in lilac dresses.
- Dress bridesmaids' hair with floral-and-lace white bonnets, placed on the back of the head and tied with large bows under the chin.
- Add gloves, lace hankies, small purses, parasols, and lace fans.

Flower Girl

- Dress the flower girl in a princess-style dress in material of your choice, with a square eyelet-lace ruffle neckline and bodice and a large bustle bow tied in back. (A princess-style dress has no waistline seam. The cut follows the body and then flares out into a full skirt that, in this case, stops just below the knee.)
- Add tights and Victorian boots.
- Tie the flower girl's hair with a large satin bow, or add a round, flat-crowned, brimmed straw hat trimmed with a wreath of green leaves.
- Give her a small basket filled with flowers to drop along her path.

Ring Bearer

Small boys were often included as pages or train bearers in Victorian weddings. Yesterday's page will be today's ring bearer:

- Dress the ring bearer in a favorite Victorian outfit: a red velvet suit with knee-length trousers.
- Place the rings in the ring bearer's breast pocket, and have him carry an old-fashioned toy hoop, a common toy of the era. (If possible, have the ring bearer push the hoop down the aisle with a stick.)

Ceremony

Wedding Site

Consider one of these location ideas when choosing a wedding site:

—Victorian-style church, house, or mansion

—Boathouse, garden pavilion, or elegant hotel

—Victorian bed and breakfast

Decor

- Make a Victorian photo gallery of the bride's and groom's relatives. Be sure to label the photos with each subject's identity.

- Set up velvet stuffed chairs and couches for elegant seating.

- In outdoor settings, set up a gazebo, and, if available, fill a pond with water lilies and swans.

- Add the following lavish and dainty touches:

—Flower garlands

—Antique picture frames, doilies, and ribbons

—Antique dolls and toys

—Lovebirds in a cage surrounded by greenery

Music

Hire a string ensemble and harpist to play selections from Tchaikovsky, Ravel, Beethoven, Brahms, and Bach.

Special Touches

Shower the bride and groom with rice or confetti:

- Give the guests decorative containers, such as handmade silk roses, filled with rice (or birdseed, if outside), and doily cones filled with confetti.

- Place rice (or birdseed) in the centers of delicate handkerchiefs, bring the sides up, and tie with beautiful ribbons.

Transportation

Provide a horse and carriage for carrying the bride to the ceremony, transporting the newly married couple to the celebration, or whisking the bride and groom off to their honeymoon.

Reception

Area Decor

Hold the reception in the same location as the ceremony.

Table Decor

Decorate tables with Victorian charm:

- Drape tables with layers of lace tablecloths and toppers.
- Sprinkle tabletops with fragrant rose petals.
- Fill teapots with bouquets of rosebuds to use as centerpieces.
- Place silver finger bowls next to place settings.
- Set up silver or china tea sets with decorative cups and saucers at each table. Add decorative napkin rings and pretty cloth or lace napkins. If you don't have enough tea sets, set up a tea service on one or more buffet tables.
- Set out crystal wine dispensers filled with claret, a favorite Victorian red Bordeaux wine, at each table or on a buffet table.
- Set out Victorian-looking place cards.
- Place doilies under dinner plates for decoration. They also make pretty decorative accents when placed on serving plates under dry foods, such as cake, dinner rolls, finger sandwiches, and so on.
- Accent place settings with Victorian sachets filled with potpourri.
- Fold napkins into swan shapes.
- If possible, create an intimate atmosphere by surrounding tables with padded and upholstered Victorian chairs and couches.

Favors

- Candy or potpourri layered in netting and tied with a satin ribbon

Guest Book

Provide an antique-looking guest book for guests to sign.

Entertainment

Tossing the bride's bouquet and garter are common modern traditions that date back to shoe, stocking, garter, and flower tossing of early centuries. (These rituals were usually performed in the bridal sleeping chamber.) For your Victorian celebration, choose one of the older customs, tossing a slipper, shoe, or stocking. Or, have the bridesmaids toss flowers into a top hat outstretched by the groom. Following are additional entertainment suggestions with a Victorian flair:

- Have croquet games on the lawn.
- Provide guests with bicycles built for two.
- Play parlor games.
- Listen to a string quartet playing classical tunes from Tchaikovsky, Ravel, Debussy, Beethoven, Mendelssohn, Brahms, and Bach.
- Dance in a gazebo. (Provide dance cards for a special touch.)
- Have a Victorian-clad entertainer recite a Victorian poem or other reading selection.
- Have a musician play an old-fashioned Victorian pump organ.
- Try this flower table-assignment mixer: Use ribbons to attach table-assignment cards to individual flower stems. In addition to the guests' names, the cards should include the flowers' meanings. For example, carnation means love, gardenia—joy, lily of the valley—happiness, orchid—beauty, iris—good health, magnolia—love of nature, daisy—early riser, and so on. Make sure that each table's centerpiece corresponds to a specific flower. (If using small tea tables, place a few stems of corresponding flowers in a small vase.) Place the tagged flower stems loosely into one or more vases near the door and distribute one to each guest. Ask guests to match their flower to a corresponding table.
- Entertain single female guests with the Victorian bridal-attendant cake-pull custom. (See Cake.)

Menu

The Victorian theme is perfect for an afternoon-tea menu. Serve the tea menu from sideboard buffets, or have Victorian-costumed waitstaff serve guests at individual tea tables.

- Small party sandwiches, such as ham, cucumber, egg salad, watercress, and so on, with the crusts removed (Cut each sandwich diagonally, from corner to corner, into four smaller sandwiches, or use cookie cutters to cut them into romantic shapes, such as flowers, hearts, or wedding bells.)
- Salmon and cream cheese pinwheel sandwiches
- Heart-shaped scones with clotted cream (or whipped butter), lemon curd, and a variety of homemade jams (If you like, serve a variety of scone flavors—current, cheese, chocolate chip, and so on.)

- Crumpets with butter and jam
- Tea cookies, such as shortbread, butter, almond, Florentine, or any other small cookies
- Small pieces of cake (such as the tiered wedding cake), pies, brownies, cheesecake, small fruit tarts, and other desserts
- Assorted fruit, cut into small pieces
- Variety of teas served with lemon, cream, and lumps of sugar (Include such favorites as Earl Grey, Darjeeling, and Kiwi-Strawberry.)
- Lemonade

Cake

Select a tiered cake, a popular choice since the Victorian ages, and consider these charming touches:

- Pass portions of the wedding cake through the wedding ring, an eighteenth-century custom stating that bachelors and spinsters who eat cake that has been passed through a wedding ring will soon be married themselves. For a modern interpretation, make an ornamental ring, about the size of a plate, by wrapping a circular wire with decorative ribbons and flowers.
- Top the cake with grandma's cake topper.
- Serve champagne in antique goblets to the bride and groom.
- Display monogrammed pastel mint patties on silver trays lined with doilies.
- Surround the wedding cake with small, decorative boxes containing pieces of wedding cake for guests to take home.
- Attach silver decorative charms to the ends of long satin ribbons. Then, place each ribbon end under the wedding cake, draping the charm ends over the table. Invite all the single females to pull a ribbon from under the cake (a Victorian cake-pull custom for providing gifts for the bride's attendants, who later hung the charms on neck chains). Then, provide cards imprinted with each charm's meaning. For example, a heart charm can signify a new love, or a book charm can signify that a studious stranger will enter her life.

Secret Wedding Mission

S hh! A secret wedding mission lurks in the shadows of love and romance. This wedding ceremony was originally inspired by the TV show *Mission Impossible,* which become more popular with the film version. This unique theme wedding is informal, and yet flashy, and allows for impromptu wedding plans. It's not for everyone, but those who choose this "secret" wedding plan will find that the fun and excitement shared with family and friends cannot be kept secret.

Invitations

Place an audio cassette tape and a file folder filled with photographs into a brown paper classified envelope. Enclose a pair of dark glasses or a black half mask. To make the audio tape, play the *Mission Impossible* theme song in the background, and record the following or similar instructions:

"Your mission, (insert name of guest or just say "wedding guest"), should you decide to accept it, is to come to the location pictured in Photograph #1 (photograph of the wedding ceremony site). It is the site of a special ceremony involving the couple pictured in Photograph #2 (bride and groom as children). Afterward, you are to go to the location pictured in Photograph #3 (wedding reception site). Your attendance is requested to help celebrate the happiest day ever by dancing, eating, and having fun. This mission is risky; expect lurking love, romance, and happiness. Please wear the enclosed dark glasses/mask to conceal your identity. This tape will self-destruct in thirty seconds."

Note: Be sure to include a printed invitation detailing the date, time, and address of ceremony and reception. You'll also need to get permission to record the theme song, but it's easy and inexpensive. (See Supplier Resource Directory, page 171.)

Guests' Dress

Instruct guests to wear traditional wedding attire, plus the dark glasses or half masks included with the invitations.

Wedding-Party Dress

Dress the entire wedding party incognito—from the bride and groom to the flower girl and ring bearer—in matching tuxes and dark glasses or black half masks.

Bridal Bouquet

Bunch tulips together into a small bouquet, wrapping the stems with white satin ribbon. Use this bouquet design for both the bride and the bridesmaids.

Flower Girl

Have the flower girl carry an envelope, marked "Confidential," filled with flower petals to scatter.

Ring Bearer

Have the ring bearer carry a large metal, flat film canister that holds the wedding rings.

Ceremony

Wedding Site

Have friends and family meet at the courthouse for this secretive ceremony.

Decor

No decorations are allowed, or needed.

Music

Play recorded music. Start with the theme from *Mission Impossible*.

Special Touches

Give guests disposable cameras and encourage candid photo taking.

Transportation

Whisk the bride and groom off to the reception site in an unmarked van or in a black stretch limousine.

Reception

Area Decor

Hold the reception in a private room of an elegant restaurant or in a warehouse, and try any or all of the following suggestions to create the appropriate atmosphere:

- Drape a small banner reading "Mission Accomplished" over the corner of a poster-sized photo of the bride and groom. (Or hang a large banner with the same words.)
- Dim the lights and have a dome-shaped, metal-workshop-like spotlight over each table. (If you like, use flashlights to illuminate the centerpiece and other items.)
- If possible, hang *Mission Impossible* movie posters on the walls.
- Use the props used in the TV videotaping sets (described in Entertainment) as part of the decor.

Table Decor

- Cover the tables with white tablecloths, and top with nightclub table lamps.
- Decorate the buffet table with a centerpiece of a TV clapboard entitled "Mission Impossible." Next to it, place a roll of audio tape with the tape all tangled up (or with a melted cassette), burnt invitations and photographs, a rubber face mask, and brown gloves.

Favors

Consider these wedding favors when planning this secret mission:

- Photo jigsaw puzzles of the wedding couple (These puzzles are an excellent party mixer and are fun to put together.)
- Wine glasses engraved with "[groom's name] and [bride's name]— Mission Accomplished."
- Photos of the bride's and groom's faces on a stick. (See Entertainment.)

Guest Book

Design a guest book to look like a TV script. Type TV-show dialogue on separate pieces of paper, place blank sheets of paper with the headline "The Players" in front, and staple the whole thing into a heavy-duty paper booklet cover. Print "[Bride and Groom's Name] Secret Wedding" on the cover. Have guests sign the blank pages.

Entertainment

- Issue secret-message seating cards, with the table designations printed in reverse. Use phrasing like, "Your mission is to report to table #12." Instruct guests to hold the cards up to a mirror to discover their table assignments.

- Play videotapes of old *Mission Impossible* episodes on television monitors or wide screens placed around the room.

- Plant disguised performers throughout the reception room. For example, have the "bartender" break into an operatic song. Have a "police officer" arrive and do a tap dance for the crowd. Maybe, "grandma" can break dance.

- Make masks out of photos of the bride's and groom's faces. Have a custom song written for the couple and place copies of the song lyrics on the backs of these masks. Pass masks out to guests and, at a designated time, have guests hold up the masks and serenade the bride and groom. (See Supplier Resource Directory, page 169.)

- Have guests produce and videotape a TV show. Hire an activity coordinator to play director, and a screenwriter to produce a TV script. Try locating the director and producer through a local college or theater group. Set up a separate area as a TV sound stage, with special lights, a mock overhead microphone, and so on. Place a video camera on a tripod, set out a clapboard, and display furniture and other props specified in the script.

- Set up a target shooting range. Use paint ball pellets to shoot human target outlines.

Menu

Your mission, should you decide to accept it, is to choose one of the following menu ideas for your wedding reception:

- Have waitstaff serve hot hors d'oeuvres and martinis on TV dinner trays.

- Hold a champagne/wine and wedding cake tasting event, hosted by a wine connoisseur and a pastry chef duo.

- Hold a wine and cheese tasting event, with an informative expert as a host.

- Provide an additional buffet table with cold hors d'oeuvres, vegetable crudités, cheese, crackers, and so on, to complement and supplement any of the above menus.

Tip: For the tasting sessions, serve small portions of each item and provide printed cards for labeling and identifying or rating items. Add this special introduction: "Your mission, should you decide to accept it, is to identify (or rate) the wines (or cheeses, cakes, and so on)." If you like, make a special videotape with a similar greeting.

Cake

Decorate a sheet cake with a movie clapboard design. Include the words, "Confidential" and "[Bride] and [Groom]—Mission Accomplished!"

Dreaming of a White Wedding— A Christmas Romance

M ake your Christmas dreams come true with a white wonderland of snow and romance. Your wedding can sparkle with the merry cheer and wonderment of the Christmas season. Envelope your guests in snowflake splendor, and treat them to the fantasies that appeal to the child in all of us.

Invitations

Make a dreamy Christmas wedding invitation with one of these ideas:

- Write these words in the invitation: "I dreamed of a white wedding full of Christmas romance; he said he dreamed of a wedding that would make me his wife."
- Print the invitation details inside a winter-wonderland-scene Christmas card.
- Enclose a white candy cane or a white Christmas tree ornament (such as a snowflake) with each invitation.
- Send each invitation in a gift box filled with imitation snowflakes.

Guests' Dress

Ask guests to wear winter white.

Wedding-Party Dress

Bride

- Choose a long, flowing, white, satin gown.
- Add a short, white imitation-fur jacket and a wide, fur-like hat.

Bridal Bouquet

Trim a large imitation-fur muff with holly and tiny silver bells.

Groom

Select a white wool tux and white bow tie. Add a mistletoe boutonniere.

Groomsmen

Dress groomsmen in white wool tuxes with white bow ties.

Bridesmaids

- Dress bridesmaids in wintry splendor in an ensemble of a white velvet blazer and a velvet floor-length skirt.
- Place small fur-like hats on their heads.
- Light up the aisle with a little holiday romance by giving each bridesmaid a battery-operated candlestick to carry.

Flower Girl

- Turn the flower girl into a sparkling snowflake creation with a white jumper, white tights, and a snowball-type fur hat.
- Have her carry a small gift box or bag containing imitation snow to scatter along the runner.

Ring Bearer

- Choose a white tux for the ring bearer.
- Have the ring bearer carry a gift-wrapped box with the rings attached to the bow.

Ceremony

Wedding Site

Hold the ceremony in a place of worship.

Decor

- Line the front of the room with candelabra stands.
- Trim pews with white poinsettias, small silver bells, and battery-operated twinkle lights.
- Make a wedding arch with white poinsettias and twinkle lights.

Music

Fill the air with Christmas music:

- Have the organist or pianist play Christmas songs before the ceremony.
- During the service, have a children's chorus sing a few carols or perform with ringing bells.
- Be sure to include the song "I'm Dreaming of a White Christmas."

Special Touches

- Have the groom wear a mistletoe boutonniere. Make sure he can easily remove it to hold it over his bride for their first married kiss.
- Shoot a cannon full of white confetti as the bride and groom exchange their wedding kiss.
- Give guests tiny bells to ring as the bridal couple leaves the ceremony site. Attach a card instructing guests to ring the bell at the reception whenever they would like the bridal couple to kiss.

Transportation

Have Santa Claus, dressed in an all-white suit, transport the bride and groom to the reception in a horse-drawn sleigh. Add wheels to the sleigh for snowless climates.

Reception

Area Decor

Hold the reception in a lodge or hotel ballroom (with a fireplace, if possible), and create your own winter wonderland:

- Decorate the ceiling of the room with twinkle lights.
- Hang white-flocked evergreen wreaths on the walls.
- Decorate a tall Christmas tree with all-white decorations.

- Enlarge black-and-white photos of the bride and groom as children (winter scenes are great, but not necessary), and display behind the head table.
- Hang mistletoe in several places around the room.

Table Decor

- Cover tables with floor-length, iridescent, white tablecloths.
- Use matching chair covers tied with silver sashes and bows.
- "Gift wrap" tables with large silver-bow centerpieces. Drape the ends of the ribbon to the floor.
- Place individual glass votive candles at each place setting.
- Wrap napkins with holly or mistletoe napkin rings.

Favors

- White English party crackers—small wrapped tubes containing small gifts, such as white candied almonds and Hershey's Chocolate Kisses, placed on each plate (These are traditionally a sign of friendship among those gathered at the table. Tie the crackers with large, white, iridescent bows, and attach place cards to each ribbon. Each cracker should be broken open by two guests, each pulling on one end.)
- Memento Christmas tree ornaments inscribed with the bride's and groom's names and wedding date (Hang these on the tree, and have Santa and his elves distribute the favors to guests as they leave.)

Guest Book

Design the guest book to resemble Santa's toy wish list.

Entertainment

- Entertain guests with Charles Dickens-type carolers.
- Hire a pianist to lead the group in Christmas carols.
- Have Santa Claus walk around and greet guests. If children will attend, have Santa give out small toys or candy canes.

Menu

Try this holiday menu:

- Lamb with mint jelly
- New potatoes

- Asparagus with hollandaise sauce and red pimento garnishes
- Spinach and tomato salad
- Eggnog
- Sparkling champagne punch (Serve during the cocktail hour. Place on a table draped with a shimmering white cloth and decorated with imitation snowflakes. Complete this display with an ice sculpture of Santa Claus.)

Cake

- Have the baker create a white cake resembling a tier of seven or eight gift boxes. Place a large cascading fondant bow on top of the "boxes."
- Place gingerbread houses and fruitcakes on either side of the cake.
- Have Santa's elves cut and serve the cake.

A Wedding of Western Romance

Western weddings are one of the most requested wedding themes and are perfect for both informal and formal affairs. A trailblaze of love sweeps through this wedding creation. So follow these easy wedding plans to "tie the knot" with western romance.

Invitations

Use a western-design invitation available from stationery suppliers. Or, create your own invitation with western flair:

- Tie a bandanna around each invitation, and place it in a straw cowboy hat.
- Use a bandanna to tie a real or toy horseshoe to each invitation.
- Send a rope tied in a love knot with each invitation. Attach a note, saying that the bride and groom plan to "tie the knot."

Guests' Dress

Include a note saying, "Step into your western garb and ride on over."

Wedding-Party Dress

Bride

Western styles have a variety of accents, such as fringe, boots, cowboy hats, western yoke cut, and so on. In addition, western wedding attire also reflects other dress and era styles. For example, Victorian fashions are popular, since the old west was populated during the Victorian era, as is depicted in the *Little House on the Prairie* dress style. Western wedding attire designs are unlimited, and the styles sometimes overlap each other. So, choose a white or ecru wedding gown or dress from the following styles:

- Victorian: Gown or dress cut or decorated with Victorian or late 1800s neckline, sleeves, and bustles, combined with western accents. (See A Victorian Wedding Tea for ideas.)

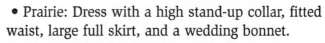

- Prairie: Dress with a high stand-up collar, fitted waist, large full skirt, and a wedding bonnet.
- Western sophisticate: Dress combining modern-day styles—including miniskirts, handkerchief hem dresses, and split shirts—with western accents.
- Traditional: Modern wedding gown accessorized with western accents.

Tip: Add a western motif, such as a silver charm cowboy hat, to the bride's garter belt.

Bridal Bouquet

For country touch, place dried wildflowers or a small bouquet of daisies into a wicker basket. Or, carry a fan with feather-and-turquoise accents.

Groom

- Choose either a frock coat or a western tuxedo bolero jacket, with or without tails. Also, a bolo tie is a must.
- Don't forget the cowboy hat and cowboy boots.
- Give the groom a simple white daisy as a boutonniere.

Groomsmen

Dress groomsmen similarly to the groom, perhaps slightly altering the style of vest, coat, or hat. Give them simple yellow daisies as boutonnieres.

Bridesmaids

- Dress bridesmaids similarly to the bride.
- Include cowboy hats and cowboy or Victorian-laced boots.
- Have each bridesmaid carry a wreath of wildflowers.

Flower Girl

- Dress the flower girl in a white skirt, shirt, and fringed vest.
- Add a cowboy hat, cowboy boots, holster, and toy guns.
- Have her carry a small rope lariat with daisy accents.

Ring Bearer

- Dress the ring bearer in white jeans, shirt, and fringed vest.
- Add cowboy boots, holster, and toy guns.
- Have the ring bearer carry the rings in a cowboy hat.

Ceremony

Wedding Site

Choose one of these locations for your wedding site:
   —Barn or stable
   —Country church
   —Event hall

Decor

- Conduct the ceremony under a love-knot wedding arch, decorated with horseshoes.
- Have guests sit on bales of hay.
- Attach wildflower bouquets to pews or end chairs, to serve as aisle markers or decorations.
- Decorate the area with a spirit of the old west:
   —Native American blankets
   —Bleached cattle skulls
   —Wagon wheels
   —Horse saddles, halters, and bridles
   —Tin lamp shades
   —Wagon wheel chandeliers
   —Native American pottery
   —Gold pans

Music

Have a fiddler perform the wedding music.

Special Touches

Give guests bandannas filled with birdseed to throw on the bride and groom.

Transportation

Transport the bride and groom in a stagecoach or hay wagon. Organize under-the-stars stagecoach or hay wagon rides during the reception. Experienced riders may choose to ride to the ceremony on horseback.

Reception

Area Decor

Hold the reception out on the country-church lawn, in a barn or stable, or in an event hall. Decorate the site similarly to the wedding ceremony site, and add the following touches:

- Decorate buffet tables with a skirting of bandanna streamers. Trim with a turquoise-bead ribbon.
- Use cowboy hats or metal campfire coffee pots as unique vases.
- Illuminate the room with candles in mason jars. (Place a layer of sand in each jar under the candle.)
- Create an unusual buffet service table: Line the bed of a country-like wagon with a red-and-white-checked or bandanna-print cloth, decoratively draping the cloth over the sides. Wrap red, white, and black satin ribbons or rope around the wheel spokes and wagon handle.
- For outdoor decor, tie large bandanna-print or red-and-white-checked cloth bows around tree trunks. (This is also a great decorative touch for the ceremony decor.)

Table Decor

- Cover tables with country quilts or red-and-white-checked tablecloths.
- Make centerpieces from black cowboy boots filled with yellow daisies or orange sunflowers.
- Make centerpieces by placing kerosene lanterns inside gold pans. Embellish this design by placing cacti around the lanterns and placing the centerpieces on bandannas.
- Wrap silverware in navy bandannas, and tie rope love knots around each napkin.
- Serve dinner on tin plates or aluminum pie tins.
- Serve coffee in tin cups.

- Write the names of famous cowboys on plastic drink glasses: Wyatt Earp, Billy the Kid, Annie Oakley, and so on.
- Toast the bride and groom with handled beer mugs.

Favors
- Tree seedlings wrapped in bandannas

Guest Book
Have guests sign a cowboy boot (shellac it later), or provide a leather-bound guest book.

Entertainment
Provide plenty of "boot-kicking" fun:
- Have each bachelor try using a lariat to rope in an available bachelorette.
- Hire a Buffalo Bill look-alike entertainer to greet guests.
- Hold a square dance.
- Conduct a campfire sing-along.
- Give country line-dance lessons.
- Hire a cowboy poet to entertain guests.
- Set up a hay bale maze.
- Rent a mechanical bull and a rodeo ropin' game.
- Hide one or more toy diamond rings in a sawdust pile. Invite children and/or adults to find the rings. Award prizes.
- Hold a horseshoe pitching contest or activity.
- Toss poker chips into cowboy hats. (Award prizes corresponding to respective hats.)
- Use squirt guns to shoot out a candle mounted on a tin (or aluminum) pie plate. Nail the pie plate to a piece of split-rail fence.
- Hold a horse race: Ask guests to step into potato or flour sacks or pillowcases, and jump to the finish line.

Menu
This informal theme calls for an informal menu. So serve a country barbecue:
- Barbecued beef and chicken
- Potato salad and coleslaw
- Corn on the cob

- Baked beans
- Buttermilk biscuits
- Coffee and marshmallows cooked over an open flame

If you hold your reception in the morning, consider having a flapjack breakfast:

- Large flapjacks (pancakes) cooked over an open flame and served with hot maple syrup (Entertain guests with a fun "Who can make the highest pancake flip?" demonstration.)
- Sausage, bacon, hash browns, and eggs-to-order
- Fruit and a variety of breakfast cereals
- Orange juice
- Toast, fresh butter, and plenty of homemade jams

Cake

Give your wedding cake a western twist:

- Place a western couple, horseshoe, or cowboy-hat cake topper on a traditional tiered cake. (Place groom's cakes, in the shapes of a horseshoe and a cowboy boot, on either side of the cake.)
- Serve a chocolate Texas sheet cake. (Everything is done "big and tall" in Texas, and this cake is a chocolate delight in a big and tall way.)
- Make a Pineapple Upside Down cake (a common western wedding dessert).
- Offer strawberry shortcake and apple dump cake. (Before baking, all ingredients are dumped into one bowl—thus, the name.)

Wedding at the Sock Hop

I nvite guests to "Bop 'till you drop at our wedding sock hop."
Everybody loves the fifties—young and old. This theme wedding will
"drive-in" to the fantastic fifties with rockin' fun and excitement. It's
a perfect way to celebrate one of the happiest days of your life.

Invitations

- Include a piece of bubble gum with each invitation.
- Attach each invitation to a bobby sock, a diary page, or a 45 RPM
  record of the 1950s era.

Guests' Dress

Include a note with the invitations: "Roll up your pant legs, dust off your
poodle skirts, and arrange your hair into a ducktail or ponytail."

Wedding-Party Dress

Bride

Since bridal fashions have not changed drastically in these years, today's
traditional bridal gown is very similar to the bridal gown of the 1950s.
Therefore, you'll likely find a bridal gown for this sock hop wedding right
off the rack, or design one of your own:

- Select a gown with a simple bodice, scoop neckline, and cap sleeves.
  Choose a just-below-the-knee skirt, standing out over layers and layers
  or crinoline. Accessorize with long gloves and a large satin bow headpiece holding a shoulder-length veil.
- Choose a floor-length gown with long, fitted sleeves and an intriguing
  sweetheart neckline. Add a traditional crown headpiece with a long veil
  and a dramatic cathedral train.

- Design a fun a unique gown with a 1950s prom-dress influence:

    —Sleeveless gown with a very full, taffeta skirt, and a fitted, lace bodice (Consider recycling a vintage prom dress.)

    —Fabric roses in a line all around the skirt, at about thigh level

    —Choker of fabric roses

    —Long, white gloves

    —For long hair, a ponytail with a fabric rose accent at the rubber band

    —For short hair, a headband of fabric roses

Bridal Bouquet

Choose one of these traditional fifties' bridal bouquets:

—Crescent-shaped bouquet

—Round nosegay

Groom

- Dress the groom in a white tuxedo coat, black tuxedo slacks, and a black cummerbund and bow tie.
- Give him a pink carnation boutonniere.

Groomsmen

Dress groomsmen similarly to the groom.

Bridesmaids

- Dress bridesmaids in variously colored pastel, taffeta dresses that hang just below the knees.
- Adorn their hair with matching sheer, wide-brimmed hats with long ribbon bows.
- Add wrist-length white gloves.
- Dye pumps to match each bridesmaid's dress.
- Have them carry high-school yearbooks.

Flower Girl

- Dress the flower girl to resemble a bobby-soxer, in a cardigan sweater, a pink poodle skirt, bobby socks, and saddles shoes.
- Arrange her hair in a ponytail.
- Have the flower girl carry an old-fashioned soda glass, complete with a straw. She can dip into this "dessert" for rose petals to drop along the aisle.

Ring Bearer

- Costume the ring bearer in rolled-up jeans, T-shirt, and a leather jacket.
- Slick back hair into a ducktail.
- Secure rings onto a vinyl record.

Wedding Site

Hold the wedding in a traditional site of worship, or get married in a high-school gymnasium.

Decor

Make a wedding arch with Hula-Hoops (for very informal weddings only).

Music

Hire a school band to march down the aisle.

Special Touches

- Recruit local high-school cheerleaders to perform a cheer for the bride and groom. Give pom-poms to the guests, and invite them to chant along.
- Make Hula-Hoops available to the guests at the reception. Each time someone whirls a hoop, the bride and groom are to kiss. The longer the hula, the longer the kiss.

Transportation

Transport the bride and groom from the wedding site to the reception site (if they are in different locations) in a '57 Chevy or a Pink Cadillac.

Reception

Area Decor

Hold the reception in a high-school gymnasium, or create your own gymnasium atmosphere in a hotel ballroom or event site:

- Hang up pink, gray, and white balloons.
- Set up a soda fountain backdrop.
- Decorate the walls with records, leather coats, poodle skirts, and fifties celebrity photos.

Table Decor

- Cover tables with alternating pink and gray tablecloths.
- Make floral ice-cream soda arrangement centerpieces by placing white carnations in soda glasses, the blooms just peeking over the edge. Add straws and miniature red carnations for the cherries.
- Use miniature Pink Cadillacs as centerpieces.
- Make vases out of saddle shoes or roller skates. Put a glass inside a sock and place the glass inside a shoe. Fill the glass with water and add fresh flowers. (If using roller skates, rig them to prevent them from rolling off the table.)
- Use sunglasses as napkin holders.
- Turn vinyl albums (not the paper cover but the 33-1/3 RPM vinyl disk) into serving bowls: Place each record on top of a metal bowl and put into a hot oven for just a few minutes, until the record shapes itself along the sides of the bowl. Don't bake it too long, or it will completely melt onto the bowl. Lift out of the bowl and cool. *Caution:* Be sure to bake the records in a well-ventilated area.
- If possible, set up diner booths with jukeboxes on the tables.

Favors

- Polaroid favors (See Entertainment.)
- Pom-poms (See Special Touches.)
- Sunglasses (See Table Decor.)

Guest Book

Choose one of these novel ideas for your guest book:
—Large mural hung on the gymnasium wall
—High-school yearbook with extra pages for signing
—Autograph book

Entertainment

- Hire a deejay to spin fifties records.
- Hire a fifties dance band.
- Rent a jukebox.
- Lead guests in the bunny hop.
- Have the waitstaff dress as fifties carhops. They can wear roller skates to serve guests.
- Hire an Elvis impersonator to stroll through the crowd.
- Rent a pink Cadillac for Polaroid photo opportunities. A soda jerk and a carhop character are also fun for photo opportunities.
- Tell guests to guess the number of gum balls contained in jars placed on each table. (Award prizes to the most-accurate guessers.)
- Hold Hula-Hoop, lip-sync, and bubble-gum-blowing contests.
- For a fun seating assignment activity, match song-title name tags to corresponding table signs. Make table signs by placing 45 RPM records upright in table-number stands. Use such songs as Elvis Presley's "Blue Suede Shoes," the theme from *Happy Days,* and so on.

Menu

The fifties were a time of malt shops and drive-ins. So serve the favorites:
- Cheeseburgers and French fries
- Cherry cokes with peanuts
- Shakes and malts
- Potato chips and dips

Cake

Have a baker design a wedding cake in the shape of a jukebox, record, or hamburger.

Roaring Twenties Wedding Speakeasy

T he fascination with the youthful and somewhat-rebellious jazz age never ceases. We're intrigued with gangster and prohibition stories, as well as the giddy parties, night-clubbing, and wild pursuit of excitement. This light-hearted wedding theme adds a fun and jazzy touch to your romantic day.

Invitations

Choose one of these bootleg versions of the traditional wedding invitation:

- Feature a photo of the bride and groom, dressed in twenties costumes and standing next to a 1920s Packard, in each invitation.
- Send a bottle of champagne with a private label printed with invitation details.
- Print the invitation details on the label of a 33-1/3 RPM record.
- Include special instructions to guests: "The password to enter the speakeasy is 'love.'"

Guests' Dress

Ask guests to come dressed in 1920s attire. Or, instruct them to wear traditional wedding attire, and provide them with decorative headbands (for the women) and toy machine guns or felt fedoras (for the men) at the reception.

Wedding-Party Dress

Bride

- Choose a dress that is the hallmark of twenties fashion: the boyish straight dress—waistless, bustless, and belted around the hips. Remembered mostly for its short, knee-length design, the style actually consisted of several lengths over the years, including floor-length and intermission (short in the front and long in the back). Choose your preferred length.

- Add low-strapped, pointy-toed pumps.
- Complete the look with a traditional chaplet head-piece—a band of wax orange blossoms holding a single piece of lace-trimmed veil fabric. The chaplet is worn just above the eyes, capping the veil fabric to the head. The veil flows over the shoulders and to the floor. The general unwritten rule of the twenties was the shorter the dress, the longer the veil. You may also prefer a popular modern headpiece—a headband with veiling.

Bridal Bouquet

Recreate a twenties bridal bouquet. The bouquets were massive, with long-stemmed flowers, such as lilies and orchids. It was also popular to include love-knot-tied trailing ribbons.

Groom

- Choose formal dress for the groom. Formal wear has not changed drastically since the twenties, and you will be able to rent one of the following styles at a local tux shop:
  —Tailcoat (worn with a white waistcoat and white bow tie)
  —Dinner jacket (worn with either a dark-colored or white waistcoat)
  —Cutaway coat (worn with striped gray trousers, a waistcoat, an ascot tie, and gray gloves and spats)
- Whichever ensemble you choose, complete it with a black top hat.
- If you prefer twenties day wear, rent a suit from a costumer, purchase a suit from a vintage clothing shop, or have a tailor recreate a twenties suit. Following are two styles to consider:
  —Jazz suit: a pin-striped suit with narrow shoulders, shaped body lines—with or without a waist seam—and tapered trousers (Add a felt, rolled-brim fedora and a flower boutonniere.)
  —Traditional suit: double-breasted, four-buttoned jacket with wide lapels, and full-cut, cuffed trousers (Add a felt, rolled-brim fedora, spats, and a flower boutonniere.)

Groomsmen

Dress groomsmen similarly to the groom. If you like, choose suits that are a different color than the groom's.

Bridesmaids

- Choose chic flapper dresses trimmed with rows of fringe. For formal weddings, a sheer, ivory lace or blush-toned satin dress may be more appropriate.
- Accent the ensemble with a very long bead necklace.
- Add the popular flapper headband, worn across the forehead and decorated with a side feather.
- Or, choose a 1920s cloche hat, which covers the whole head and ears very tightly.
- Have bridesmaids carry large ostrich fans.

Flower Girl

- Dress the flower girl similarly to the bridesmaids.
- Give her a small drawstring purse holding flower petals to drop along the aisle.

Ring Bearer

- Dress the ring bearer similarly to the groomsmen.
- For an informal touch, give the ring bearer a prop bottle of bootleg gin with a ribbon and rings attached.

Ceremony

Wedding Site

Hold the ceremony in a large, early-century mansion.

Decor

- Rent 1920s antiques from a dealer to accent the room.
- Decorate with tall candelabra stands and flower garlands.

Music

Play the wedding march on an antique Victrola (substitute a recording, if necessary).

Special Touches

Fill empty liquor bottles with rice. Pass around the bottles, and have guests help themselves to handfuls of rice to throw on the bride and groom.

Transportation

Escort the bride and groom to the ceremony and away to the honeymoon in a 1920s Packard.

Area Decor

Meet wedding guests in a secret location speakeasy. A mansion basement or a hideaway nightclub would make a nice site. Include these details:

- Have a gangster character guard the door with a toy machine gun. Have him ask each guest for the secret password to gain entry.
- At the entrance, add a prop door with a small peephole for checking out the clientele.
- Dim the lighting to create a secret-hideaway atmosphere.
- Rent antiques to decorate the room.
- Fill an old claw-foot bathtub with ice and bottles of champagne, brews, and wine. Add a few bathtub-gin prop bottles.
- Label bar items as hooch, bathtub gin, red ink (homemade wine), bootleg, moonshine, and so on.

Table Decor

- Cover cocktail tables with white linen cloths.
- Wrap long flapper bead necklaces around crisp, white linen napkins.
- Float gardenias in large brandy snifters as centerpieces. Place round mirrors under the snifters.
- Place small votive candles at each place setting or around the centerpieces.
- Attach place cards to cigars and/or cigarette holders at each place setting.

Favors

- Private-label, bootleg bottles of champagne or wine, with the bride's and groom's names and the wedding date on the labels
- Cigars banded with the wedding couple's names and wedding date (Hold a cigar-smoking activity in a private room.)

Guest Book

Have guests sign an elaborately framed piece of poster board. First frame the poster board with a mat covered with 1920s photos. Then frame the whole thing with a large, decorative frame.

Entertainment

Include entertainment to provide that jazz-age feeling:

- Provide a dance band and a jazz band performance.
- Give Charleston dance lessons.
- Set up an old-time photo studio. Provide period furniture, decor, costumes, and props for black-and-white photos.
- Stage a tap dance review.
- Have entertainers, who at first appear to be part of the crowd, get on table tops and perform the Charleston.
- Play casino games.
- Conduct a road rally.
- Hold a croquet tournament. Stencil croquet mallets with the bride's and groom's names and wedding date.
- Stage a raid in which FBI or local police characters round up the suspects and place them behind bars for an instant photo opportunity.

Menu

Serve a speakeasy-simple buffet:

- Ham and cheese sandwiches
- Salads
- Chips and pretzels

Note: If you choose a mansion over a nightclub for your venue, provide a full dinner buffet.

Cake

- Serve guests slices of jelly-roll cake.

Take a Magic Carpet Ride Wedding

Take a magic carpet ride to the land of veiled enchantment for a wedding filled with Middle Eastern mystique and romance. Relive the fantasy of Aladdin as he grants your wedding wishes with a dream-come-true wedding celebration. There's no need to buy plane tickets for guests, just invite them to your very own palace for this fascinating wedding celebration.

Invitations

Invite guests with an Aladdin-like touch:

- Write invitation details on, or attach details to, an inflatable magic lamp.
- Write invitation details on a scroll, insert into a plastic bottle, and seal with a cork.
- Include a special note to guests: "Bring three wishes for the wedding couple."

Guests' Dress

Add "Black Tie" to the wedding invitations.

Wedding-Party Dress

Bride

Dress the bride in Middle Eastern mystique. Choose a Turkish-inspired costume, or design your own:

- Dress the bride in purple silk bloomers: full ankle-length trousers gathered at the ankles.
- Top the bloomers with a gold silk, long coat with long bell sleeves. The top of the coat should be tightly fitted and secured with many buttons. From the hip downward, the coat should be open in the front and flared out on each side.

- Add a Middle Eastern headdress, a yashmak, covering the face. Take two squares of white sheer silk trimmed with gold embroidering. Fold diagonally, and arrange over a small gold cap. The first folded square is placed over the head with the bias fold well down over the forehead. The second folded square covers the lower part of the face, revealing only the eyes. Secure the ends of the veils by tying them into a knot or by using hat or hair pins.
- Complete the look with gold slippers.

Bridal Bouquet

Further hide the face behind a fan of turquoise peacock feathers.

Groom

- Clothe the groom in a sultan's costume: long white bloomers, hose, and slippers.
- Add a plum shirt with a round neck and very full sleeves, a broad gold sash, and a short white bolero jacket.
- Top the ensemble with a long flowing cloak held together at the neck with a large jewel button and a large, puffy turban (accented with another jewel and feather).

Groomsmen

Dress groomsmen similarly to the groom, but without the cloak, or dress them in classic black tuxes and white turban headdresses.

Bridesmaids

- Dress bridesmaids in long, straight, sleeveless gowns with empire, jeweled waists made with silver-colored cloth.
- Have bridesmaids carry a "magic carpet" made of roses, or other flowers, to drape near the wedding couple.

Flower Girl

- Dress the flower girl in an *I Dream of Jeannie*-type costume, with a cropped top and sheer harem pants.
- Have her carry a silk scarf full of "jewels" to spread along the bridal path.

Ring Bearer

- Dress the ring bearer in a sultan's costume.
- Have the ring bearer carry the rings tied to a magic lantern.

Wedding Site

Create a palace atmosphere in an elaborately decorated ballroom.

Decor

- Hang an Aladdin's castle backdrop behind the head table.
- Drape the ceiling with sheer and colorful fabrics.
- Suspend a magic flying carpet from the ceiling, along with a genie cutout.
- Set up a Persian reflection pool.
- Cover the area with plenty of palm trees and plants.
- Show an *Aladdin* cartoon or movie on a tent wall.
- On other walls, shine gobos of camels and palm trees.
- Illuminate a black-tent ceiling with twinkle lights to resemble stars.
- Place a key-hole-shaped palace archway on a riser. Have the bride and groom exchange wedding vows in front of this palace doorway.

Music

Play recorded Middle Eastern music, or hire a Middle Eastern musical ensemble. Contact a local belly dancer entertainer for music sources.

Special Touches

- Throw colorful paper streamers at the happy couple as their marriage is announced.
- Dress wedding greeters in *I Dream of Jeannie*-type and Sultan costumes. Have the characters give out plastic or glass corked bottles with candy. Add special labels with the wedding couple's names and wedding date.

Transportation

For a dramatic touch, have costumed servants carry the bride down the aisle on a large Persian carpet.

Reception

Area Decor

Hold the reception at the same site as the wedding ceremony.

Table Decor

Cover the tables in Middle Eastern romance:

- Elaborately drape the tables in royal colors of your choice.
- Use magic lamps and *I Dream of Jeannie*-type bottles for centerpieces.
- Place plumed sultan's hats on pedestal stands as centerpieces.

Favors

- Plastic or glass corked bottles of candy (See Special Touches.)
- Pistachios wrapped in colorful scarves
- Miniature or chocolate magic lamps
- Plush toy camels
- Colorful scarves
- Cassettes of Middle Eastern music
- Framed Polaroid photos (See Entertainment.)
- Small *Aladdin* children's books
- Disney's *Aladdin* figures, key chains, and so on

Guest Book

Have guests sign an antique-looking scroll or a "magic" carpet.

Entertainment

- Have belly dancers perform for the crowd.
- Hire strolling magicians, stilt walkers, snake charmers, sword swallowers, jugglers, and so on. (Ask the entertainers to dress in Middle Eastern costumes.)
- Set up Polaroid photo spots. Simulate lying on a bed of nails, riding a camel, rubbing a magic lamp, or hiding in a genie's bottle.
- Show *Aladdin* movies or cartoons and *I Dream of Jeannie* TV episodes on large screens.
- Collect and present wedding wishes, brought by guests, to the bride and groom during a special toast.

Menu

The following main dishes will give your guests a taste of the Middle East:

- Shish kebab
- Moussaka (eggplant, ground lamb or beef, cheese, and seasonings wrapped in phyllo dough)
- Falafel
- Kibbeh burghal (wheat pie)
- Kibbeh balls with yogurt sauce

Add sides of:

- Dolma (stuffed grape leaves)
- Hamith helu (stewed dry fruit)
- Yellow rice
- Figs and olives
- Pita bread

For dessert:

- Fresh fruits
- Fancy trays of candies
- Baklava and Arabic coffee

Cake

Design the cake to resemble a Persian reflecting pool, or decorate a giant tiered cake with marzipan fruit.

L'amour-on-Canvas Wedding Picnic

Whirl guests off to the country or to a mountainside for an afternoon wedding picnic of croissants, painter's easels, and savoir faire! This theme is wonderful for outdoor weddings—in a meadow, park, or mountainside—but it can also be staged indoors. Fresh air, sunshine, and romantic French ambiance permeate this romantic "painting of love" event.

Invitations

- Print invitation details on painter's palettes. Dot palettes with different-colored paint swirls. Attach paintbrushes.
- Write invitation details on art-reproduction note cards or postcards. Attach paintbrushes.
- Include this French comment in the invitation: *"Respondez si'l vous plait"* ("Please respond").

Guests' Dress

Suggest dressy-casual picnic wear.

Wedding-Party Dress

Bride

- Create a French painting of love by dressing the bride in a crisp white sundress.
- Frame this pretty picture-bride with a large, wide-brimmed hat.

Bridal Bouquet

Make a bridal bouquet with nature's beauty and a painter's palette: Attach red, blue, green, yellow, and white carnations on an artist's palette to look like dabs of paint.

Groom

Dress the groom in a suave black ensemble, including turtleneck, slacks, sport coat, and French beret.

Groomsmen

Dress groomsmen similarly to the groom.

Bridesmaids

- Have each bridesmaid wear a brightly colored summer shift. Choose a different color for each bridesmaid, such as red, blue, green, or yellow.
- Add a straw hat trimmed with a ribbon that matches the dress.
- Have each bridesmaid carry a single long-stemmed flower matching the color of her dress. Attach the stems to large artist's paintbrushes (point-side up). Secure the flowers with floral wire in a few places, covering the wire with florist's tape. Then, wind a ribbon along the handle, leaving wide spaces to reveal the paintbrush handle.

Flower Girl

- Dress the flower girl in a painter's smock and a black French beret.
- Have her carry a small paint bucket filled with flower petals to toss on the bridal path.

Ring Bearer

- Dress the ring bearer in a painter's smock and a black French beret.
- Slip the wedding rings over the handle of a large artist's brush. (You may want to attach them in some way, in case the ring bearer swings the paintbrush.)

Ceremony

Wedding Site

Hold a beautiful landscape-painting wedding on a mountainside, next to a lily pond, in the park, in a meadow or open field, or in your own indoor park created with set decor. For outdoor sites, be sure to provide tents or awnings, in case of rain.

Decor

Lay red-and-white-checkered tablecloths on the ground for guest seating. (Provide chairs for older guests.) Make alternative plans for poor weather:

- Lay a wool or heavy blanket on the ground under the tablecloth, to absorb any moisture.
- Set up a festive tent or awning area for the wedding festivities. On a clear day, the tent will reflect the changing patterns of sunlight and shadows. On a rainy day, the tent will protect guests from the weather.

Note: The picnic atmosphere can also be re-created under the protection of a roof and four walls.

Music

Play some romantic Parisian melodies.

Special Touches

Give each guest a miniature paint can filled with one of four or five bright colors of confetti (one color per can) to throw on the happy couple after the ceremony. Decorate the outside of the paint cans with a wedding inscription.

Transportation

Transport the wedding party and wedding guests to the wedding site from a central location in town. Use small, European cars, such as Volvos or vintage Volkswagen Beetles. Lay French berets, one for each guest, on the seats of the automobiles beforehand. Play French music during the ride.

Reception

Area Decor

Hold the reception at the same site as the ceremony.

Table Decor

- Next to each checkered tablecloth on the ground, lay a wicker picnic basket filled with checkered napkins, wine glasses, wine, and lunch for each "table." Or, give each guest an individual small wicker basket, with handle, lined with a red-and-white-checked napkin.

- Fill Perrier water bottles with daisies as centerpieces.
- Set up a painter's easel with a tablet, paints, brushes, magic markers, and crayons (and painter's smocks, if you like) near each area.

Favors
- Small bags of candy decoratively tied to the ends of artist's paintbrushes
- Red-and-white-checked napkins (Attach a note with each napkin inviting guests to wrap a piece of cake in the napkin to take home.)

Guest Book
Set up a special easel, with a large tablet and colorful magic markers, near the ceremony area. Encourage guests to sign their names on this special guest book.

Entertainment
Entertain guests with French artiste flair:
- Hire actors, dressed as French artists (in painter's smocks, French berets, and charcoal mustaches) to greet guests as they arrive at the picnic wedding site. The greeters can hold a variety of French props, including artist's palettes, framed oil paintings, or even French poodles.
- Play some romantic Parisian melodies.
- Encourage the picnic groups to draw their own artistic creations using the provided easels and paint supplies. Designate an activity leader to direct the first artist to draw part of the painting. Then, have each subsequent artist add something new to the painting. Frame the finished and dried artwork as a gift to the bride and groom.
- Hire a couple of art teachers to give informal instructions. For a little humor, blindfold the bride and groom and have them paint one picture together.
- Provide face painters.
- Costume the waitstaff as artists, and have them pass hors d'oeuvres to guests from painter's palette trays.

Menu
Delicate French touches will surely appeal to your guests' taste palates:
- Individual quiche squares or triangles
- Brie, pâté, and caviar

- Various rémoulades (cold sauces), French bread, and grapes
- Bottles of French wine

Note: For a heavier lunch, add Croissant sandwiches, raw vegetables, and pasta salad.

Cake

Arrange cream puffs and other French pastries in the shape of a tiered wedding cake.

Love Boat Wedding Cruise

Plan a nautical celebration to make your guests feel like they have stepped aboard the Love Boat for a wedding cruise on the sea of love. This breezy and romantic theme combines vacation-like fun with the allure of the sea. It lends itself to an elegant formal affair, as well as a fun-loving casual bash.

Invitations

Many unique invitation ideas would be perfect for this wedding cruise theme:

- Design invitations to look and read like passports.
- Attach invitations to Hawaiian leis. (Or, write invitation details on a few strips of paper, and weave the strips into the leis.)
- Enclose toy sailboats, miniature life preservers, or captain's sailor hats.
- Place invitations inside brass photo frames.
- Print invitation details on private-label champagne bottles.

Guests' Dress

For a fun and informal wedding, tell guests to wear casual vacation wear—the tackier, the better. Inform guests that there will be a contest for the "Tackiest Tourist Costume."

Wedding-Party Dress

Bride

- Choose a bridal dress with a nautical touch. Start with floor-length white-satin, full culottes. Add a hip-length tunic with a wide sailor's collar and a white flowing organza tie.
- Tie the bride's hair back at the nape of the neck with a large white organza bow, attaching some short bridal netting to the bow.

Bridal Bouquet

Have a florist make a wreath of magnolias around a small life preserver prop.

Groom

Dress the groom in a formal white Navy-like dress uniform, with a captain's hat.

Groomsmen

Dress groomsmen in less-formal Navy deck-style uniforms: white bell bottoms, white sailor shirts with collar, blue sailor ties, and white sailor hats.

Bridesmaids

• Have bridesmaids wear shorts-length sailor-style culotte-skirt dresses with sailor colors, blue nautical trim, and blue cloth ties.

• Adorn their hair with blue bows.

• Create a sea of color with small, blue bridesmaids' bouquets made with blue pansies, Spanish bluebells, blue poppies, and other blue flowers.

Flower Girl

• Dress the flower girl in a navy sailor skirt and shirt, adding a navy sailor tam.

• Have the flower girl carry a bouquet of red heart-shaped helium balloons.

Ring Bearer

• Dress the ring bearer in a navy sailor suit made from a pair of shorts, shirt, and a white sailor hat.

• Place the wedding rings in a toy boat for the ring bearer to carry.

Ceremony

Wedding Site

Choose a nautical-themed wedding site:

—On an actual docked cruise ship

—At a historical boat site

—At a restaurant with a nautical theme

—On a yacht

—At a seaside or lakeside restaurant with a spectacular waterfront view

—On a lake or seashore beach

—At a country club, hotel, or home poolside

Decor

Create your own cruise ship atmosphere in a hotel or reception site ballroom:

- Decorate the area with portholes, ship's bells, life preservers, and so on.

- Stack vintage luggage, including steamer trunks, hat boxes, and a wicker bird cage into a pile. Add a sign, "Welcome to [bride's name]'s and [groom's name]'s Love Boat Wedding Cruise."

- Build a ship's deck with railing, portholes, deck furniture, and life preservers. This area will be perfect for the bride and groom to exchange wedding vows. It will also serve as a photo opportunity for guests.

- Label a large life preserver "SS Love Boat Wedding Cruise." Label another with "[bride's name] and [groom's name]."

- Suspend international and nautical flags from the ceiling.

- Hang a steamship backdrop on the stage.

- Set up a fog machine, and play foghorn sounds near the ship's smoke stack for a dramatic effect.

- Have the bridal party walk up a plank built on the stage.

- Contact a specialty lighting company to create ocean-wave reflections using gobo lighting.

Music

Play the theme from *The Love Boat* TV show.

Special Touches

- Give guests soap bubbles to blow at the wedding couple.
- Hand out confetti party-blaster horns, available commercially.

Transportation

Transport the bride and groom to or from the wedding site in a speedboat or rowboat.

Reception

Area Decor

Hold the reception at the same site as the ceremony.

Table Decor

Create sea-faring table decor:

- Cover tables in alternating sea-blue and white tablecloths.
- Choose tablecloths in varying shades of blue (to create the illusion of waves).
- Top tables with centerpieces made from champagne bottles, captain's sailor hats, and miniature life preservers.
- Make decadent duo centerpieces by dipping the bottoms of champagne bottles in chocolate and letting them dry (wrap the bottles in food-grade shrink-wrap first). Place the bottles on pieces of crumpled blue cellophane over mirror squares, or in silver champagne buckets. If you place the bottles on ice, protect the chocolate with cellophane.
- Make sailor-hat centerpieces by trimming the brims of sailor hats with thin red and blue ribbons. Attach red, white, and blue helium balloons.
- Make centerpieces by enlarging reproductions of vintage passenger-steamship luggage tags. Mount the reproductions on foam core and attach to perpendicular bases.
- Use one of these unique ideas as table seating assignments:
  - —Write numbers that correspond to tables on the bottoms of plastic ducks. Float the ducks in a child-sized pool, and let guests pick a floating duck for their table assignment.
  - —Place cruise-ship deck names on each table, such as "promenade," "bridge," and so on, that correspond to guests' seating assignment tickets.

Favors

No vacation-like wedding ceremony would be complete without souvenirs:

- Sailor hats inscribed with the bride's and groom's names and wedding date
- Personalized champagne bottles or glasses
- LifeSaver candies (distributed from souvenir carts)
- Small inexpensive compasses

Guest Book

Have guests sign in on a captain's logbook.

Entertainment

- Hire actors to portray the various characters from *The Love Boat* TV show—captain, purser, and other cruise-ship personnel.
- Have a Jamaican band greet guests at embarking.
- Hire a deejay to play cruisin' tunes and to lead guests in some cruise-ship fun.
- Include a Hula-Hoop and limbo contest.
- Play sailor-hat musical chairs. Instead of removing a chair during each play, place a sailor hat on a chair. Guests are instructed to sit on a chair without a hat.
- Make paper boats, and conduct a regatta.
- Offer a nautical toast to the bride and groom: "Here's to the bride and groom, may the compass of love guide you through the high seas of marriage."
- Christen the bridal couple's love boat with a bottle of champagne by breaking the bottle against the real (or prop) boat.
- Toast the bridal couple with champagne in champagne flutes with chocolate-dipped rims.

Menu

Cruise ships are known for their abundant buffets, so provide plenty of everything:

- Sea-food buffet, including a variety of lobster, crab, shrimp, fish, oyster, clam, and other seafood dishes (Serve this buffet on a table made from a rowboat.)
- Ham, beef, and turkey carving stations

- Bread buffet with a variety of muffins, breads, corn bread, biscuits, scones, and so on
- Salad bar with green, macaroni, carrot, fruit, and other salads
- Elaborate cheese and fruit buffet
- Flaming dessert station and a dessert buffet laden with such pasty delights as cakes, pies, tarts, cheesecakes, brownies, cookies, and other rich treats
- Exotic drinks, such as Mai Tai's and Piña Coladas

Tip: International food stations would also work well for this theme— Italian food station, Asian, Mexican, and so on.

Cake

- Have the baker design a cruise-ship cake.
- Place an anchor-shaped cake topper on a tiered cake.
- Make heart-shaped cakes to use as groom's cakes.

Love at the Mardi Gras Ball

C elebrate your wedding with a Mardi Gras masquerade ball. The bride and groom will rule as king and queen of the grand celebration filled with nonstop festive activity, excitement, and fun. Integrate the Mardi Gras colors into all aspects of your wedding: purple (for justice), green (for faith), and gold (for power).

Invitations

- Send a decorative Mardi Gras masquerade mask and Mardi Gras beads with each invitation.

Guests' Dress

Attach a note with each invitation asking guests to "Come to the wedding ball in masquerade."

Wedding-Party Dress

Bride

- Choose a traditional silk gown with a full skirt. The gown will serve as an elegant canvas for the unique bridal bouquet.
- Top the bride's head with a gold crown, with gold beans looped down over the forehead.
- Attach a shoulder-length veil to the headpiece.

Bridal Bouquet

Create a showpiece bridal bouquet. Start with a fancy porcelain mask, and include purple, green, and gold feathers and azalea blooms. Add plenty of thin purple, gold, and green flowing ribbons.

Groom

Choose a white tux with a gold cummerbund and bow tie.

Groomsmen

Dress groomsmen in matching black tuxedos, and give each a different-colored cummerbund and bow tie—gold, green, or purple.

Bridesmaids

- Have bridesmaids wear long, straight, satin gowns in the Mardi Gras colors of purple, gold, or green. Choose dresses with cap sleeves, cut-out backs, and large flat bows at the back of the waist.

- Have bridesmaids carry decorative half-face masks on long-handled sticks. The masks should match the color of the gowns.

Flower Girl

- Dress the flower girl as a court jester in a gold, green, and purple jacquard costume.

- Have her toss beads and doubloons along the bridal path.

Ring Bearer

- Dress the ring bearer as a court jester, also, in the same colors and fabric as the flower girl.

- Have the ring bearer carry the rings attached to a velvet-tufted gold crown.

Ceremony

Wedding Site

You'll need a large site for this event with all of its activity:

- Hold the event in a high-school gymnasium.

- Set up a tent on a football field.

- Transform a hotel or event-site ballroom into New Orleans' French Quarter.

Decor

- Set up Mardi Gras velvet king and queen thrones at the head table. Place ornamental crowns and elaborate red velvet robes on each throne.
- Conduct the ceremony on a Mardi Gras float (big enough for the wedding party).
- Hang up a New Orleans street backdrop.
- Place street lamps and signs reading "Bourbon Street," "Royal Street," and "Canal Street" throughout the event site.
- Decorate walls and furniture with purple, gold, and green draping.
- Display theatrical comedy and tragedy masks.
- Throw streamers and confetti everywhere.

Music

Hire a Dixieland jazz band.

Special Touches

Throw candy, beads, and doubloons toward the happy couple after the ceremony. Be careful not to throw these items directly on the couple.

Transportation

Parade the wedding couple to the ceremony or reception on a decorated Mardi Gras float. You can also use this float for the wedding ceremony.

Reception

Area Decor

Hold the reception in the same location as the wedding ceremony.

Table Decor

Use bold and beautiful table decorations:

- Use alternating purple, gold, and green lamé tablecloths.
- For centerpieces, hang ceramic face masks decorated with large ostrich-feather headdresses on tall Lucite stands. Drape the stands with tulle and gold bead strands. Place green, gold, or purple gift-wrap grass at the base. Add scattered candy, doubloons, and Mardi Gras beads.
- Make napkin rings out of small ceramic face masks and ribbon streamers.

Favors

- Southern pralines in cellophane, tied with purple, gold, and green ribbons

Guest Book

Have guests sign a poster of the French Quarter.

Entertainment

Create a carnival-like atmosphere with show-stopping entertainment:

- Have court jesters, jugglers, and greeters in oversized papier-mâché masks greet guests at the reception area entrance.
- Have a strolling Dixieland jazz band and costumed characters lead guests in a parade to dinner.
- Hire a dance band.
- Hire face painters, clowns, jugglers, caricature artists, puppeteers, and so on.
- Play carnival games:
  —Toss Mardi Gras beads over pop bottles, and toss doubloons into crystal goblets.
  —Set up a spinning wheel numbers game. Label each number with a romantic saying, or write the numbers and corresponding sayings on a separate sign. For example, #7 could read, "True Love—You Win," #9 could read "You Lose—You're Unlucky at Love," #11 could read, "You're the Next to Get Married—You Decide, Win or Lose?" and so on. You can also attach purple, green, and gold Mardi Gras colors to some of the numbers and award prizes corresponding to the colors.
  —Set up a floating duck pond for small children.
  —Hire a carnival supply company to set up a mechanized frog jump game.
  —Rent a "stand the pop bottle with a plastic ring-on-a-string" game— guests really enjoy this one.

Menu

This theme calls for down-home southern cooking:

- New Orleans specialties: Cajun rice, seafood dishes, gumbo, jambalaya
- Southern favorites: fried chicken, hush puppies, corn on the cob, ribs, corn bread with honey butter, baked beans

- Crab cake hors d'oeuvres
- Black-eyed peas or black-eyed pea salad
- Jumbo fried shrimp, shrimp cocktails
- Fried zucchini strips
- Watermelon

Hint: Serve drinks in Pat O'Brien Restaurant hurricane glasses. (See Supplier Resource Directory, page 155.)

Cake

- Serve a "King's Cake" as your wedding cake. Traditionally, this cake is served on King Day, January 6, to kick off Mardi Gras festivities. Choose any cake you like, ice it with white icing, and decorate it with purple, green, and gold-colored sugar. Insert a tiny plastic baby into the bottom of the cake, taking care to see where it goes. According to tradition, the person who finds the baby is designated as the host/hostess of the next Mardi Gras party. Modern custom, however, designates the finder as a prize winner or as the king or queen of Mardi Gras. If you choose the second option, crown the finder with an ornate velvet crown, give them a cape and a scepter, and have them sit on a throne. Make sure to take plenty of pictures. Caution: Supervise the baby-finding, especially if children are involved, to make sure no one chokes on the toy.
- Decorate a large round coconut cake (a southern favorite) with purple, green, and gold Mardi Gras beads, doubloons, and half-face masks.
- Serve pecan pie alongside the cake.

An Old-Fashioned Ice-Cream Social Wedding

Y ou can choose a number of time periods as the setting for this old-fashioned social, from the turn of the century to the present day. No matter what the time period, celebrate this wedding with the reminiscent gaiety and merriment of days gone by. Its sweet park (or park-like) setting and delightful Sunday-afternoon-like activities are perfect for the expression of wedding love.

Invitations

- Spray paint a sugar or wafer ice-cream cone. Fill the cone with tissue paper, wrap in cellophane, and tie with a pretty ribbon. Place the cone in a gift box with the invitation.
- Write invitation details on a vintage, turn-of-the-century postcard or note card that features a bathing beauty in antique bathing clothes or a park-stroll scene.
- Send each invitation with a miniature root beer mug.
- Hand-write each invitation on social (personal) stationery.

Guests' Dress

Ask guests to come dressed in their garden-party best—picture hats, white gloves, and so on.

Wedding-Party Dress

Bride

- Choose a modern garden-party dress with hat and gloves.
- Or, select a period-inspired gown with turn-of-the-century influence: the elegance of a handsomely tailored Edwardian gown, or the smart

romance or the Gibson Girl hour-glass look (characterized by a high neck, full sleeves, and a wasp or very slim waist).

- Add a large wide-brimmed, Edwardian-style hat decorated with veiling and/or feathers.
- Wear hair in a characteristic period style: gathered high on top of the head and twisted into a bun (hair roll), with full, puffy sides and tiny curls framing the sides of the face.

Bridal Bouquet

A frilly parasol is a must for this old-fashioned wedding social.

Groom

Match the groom's outfit to the bride's.

- Choose a suit and tie (perhaps a light-colored suit or navy jacket with white slacks) to coordinate with the bride's garden-party dress.
- If you choose to dress the groom in period clothing, consult the Groom section under "A Victorian Wedding Tea" for style suggestions. Compliment a frock coat with a bowler-style hat.

Groomsmen

Dress groomsmen identically to the groom.

Bridesmaids

Dress bridesmaids in a similar style to the bride.

Flower Girl

- Dress the flower girl in a ruffled smock-like pinafore dress of the early 1900s.
- Pull her hair back into a large light-blue bow.
- Fill a small parasol with flower petals, and have her drop the petals along the bridal path.

Ring Bearer

- Dress the ring bearer in a dapper vintage-style sailor suit: reefer coat, short trousers, knee highs, and a Buster-brown-style sailor hat.
- Have the ring bearer carry the rings in an antique music box.

Ceremony

Wedding Site

Hold the ceremony in a park, or transform an indoor area into a park-like setting.

Decor

- Decorate with trees, park benches, waterfalls, lattice work, flower gardens, and birdbaths.
- For the wedding ceremony, set up a gazebo draped with flower garlands.
- Seat guests on white wooden chairs.

Music

Announce the wedding with a marching band. Dress band members in vintage costumes.

Special Touches

Fill miniature root beer mugs with birdseed to throw on the happy couple.

Transportation

- Transport the bride to the ceremony in a horse-drawn carriage. Give guests rides in this carriage during the reception. Then, use it to whisk the bride and groom away to their honeymoon.
- Motor the couple in a Model-T Ford.
- Have the bride and groom ride away on a bicycle built for two.

Reception

Area Decor

- Station several vendor carts, attended by vintage-costumed characters, throughout the area: a flower cart, a wedding-favor cart, a hot dog cart, a popcorn cart, a roasted peanuts cart, a soft pretzel cart, a candy apple cart, a cotton candy cart, and so on.

- Lay blankets on the grass and provide picnic baskets filled with lunches.
- Set up an old-fashioned bar area in a separate tent or building, and serve guests ice-cream cones and root beer floats. Have the bartender dress in a puffy-sleeved, high-necked shirt with arm garters, a red-and-white-striped vest, and a large white cloth wrapped around his waist. He can darken his hair, part it down the middle, and style it close to his scalp. And, naturally, he should sport a handlebar mustache.
- Accent the bar area with swirling bar stools, a swinging door entrance, and a large wall mirror. Hang pictures of cancan dancers on the walls.

Table Decor

- Cover small round tables with red-and-white-striped tablecloths.
- Use pastel-colored napkins.
- Create ice-cream cone napkin rings: Break a hole in the bottom of an ice-cream cone and carefully thread a napkin through the hole.
- To create other unique napkin rings, tie any of the favor ideas, such as pinwheels, ball and jack toys, and so on, to the napkins with pretty cloths or ribbons.
- Rent soda parlor chairs to place around tables.
- Make floral ice-cream soda centerpieces. Place white carnations in tall ice-cream soda glasses. Add straws and cherries (small red carnations).
- Set out geraniums planted in clay flower pots or watering cans.
- Make edible flowerpot centerpieces: Remove lids from ice-cream tubs and place them on the bottoms of the tubs. Wrap the tubs (except the tops) in floral cellophane, and secure the cellophane at the rims of the tubs with a ribbon. (The cellophane is not only decorative, but it will also help protect the tables when the ice cream melts.) Separate a number of Oreo cookies, remove the filling, and crumble the cookies on top of the ice cream to make "dirt." Then, stick a silk flower bush and a few Gummy worms into the ice cream to complete the "flowerpots." Provide each table with ice-cream scoops, so guests can enjoy this special dessert. *Note:* Place these centerpieces on the tables just as guests are seated for dinner, so the ice cream has time to thaw a bit before serving.

Favors

- Pinwheels with the bride's and groom's names and wedding date
- Ball and jack toys and bags of marbles
- Decorated favor bags with taffy candy

Guest Book

Have guests sign their names on a white-painted park bench. Later, paint the bench with a protective coating.

Entertainment

- Have ladies and gentlemen, dressed in turn-of-the-century costumes, stroll the area and greet guests. (Have one lady carry a suffragette sign.)
- Invite guests to sit in an old-fashioned barber shop. Cover them with large white sheets, and paint handlebar mustaches on their faces with grease paint. Style guests' hair in turn-of-the-century hairstyles.
- Serenade guests with a barbershop quartet.
- Set out a player piano, or hire a piano player and/or old-time banjo musicians.
- Find entertainers to walk on stilts and to ride old-fashioned, oversized, front-wheel bicycles.
- Hold a build-the-tallest-ice-cream-cone and a bubble-blowing contests.
- Organize a taffy pull and a lemonade squeeze.
- Start a bingo game.
- Play musical chairs.
- Organize a hat parade and contest, and award prizes for the most authentic, funniest, most unusual, and so on. (If doing this activity, include a note in the invitation instructing guests to wear hats. Or, provide materials at the reception for guests to make and decorate hats for the contest.)
- Hold a croquet game.
- Organize races, relays, and toss games.
- Rent tandem bicycles for guests to ride.

Menu

This casual, outdoor celebration calls for picnic-basket lunches and homemade ice cream. Also, enjoy treats from park vendors' carts.

Cake

Build a large, round, five- or six-layer chocolate cake with chocolate icing.

Crystal Carnival Wedding Ball

L ove sparkles within the crystal walls of this winter ice-palace setting. This romantic ice-castle theme adds a novel twist to an elegant ball affair. Guests will be fascinated with the sparkling splendor of this creation, and you'll be enchanted with the special wedding memories it will bring.

Invitations

Choose one of these sparkling invitation ideas:

- Have invitation details engraved onto crystal plaques.
- Send rock candy or sugar cubes with invitations.
- Enclose snowballs with invitations: cover Styrofoam balls with opalescent glitter.
- Include notes informing guests that this will be a dessert buffet reception, so they know what to expect in the form of refreshments.

Guests' Dress

Tell guests to wear white.

Wedding-Party Dress

Bride

- Choose a long, flowing, opalescent white gown.
- Top it with a white velvet, hooded cape with a fur-like or long-feather trim.

Bridal Bouquet

- Have the bride carry a fur-like or long-feather-trimmed muff. Attach battery-powered twinkle lights to the outside of the muff.

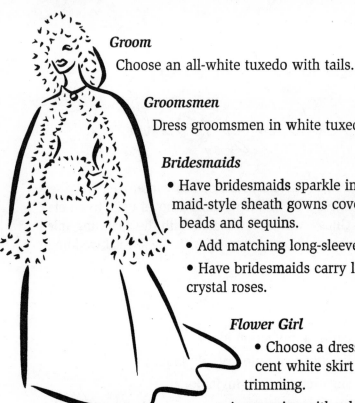

Groom

Choose an all-white tuxedo with tails.

Groomsmen

Dress groomsmen in white tuxedos (without tails).

Bridesmaids

- Have bridesmaids sparkle in crystal-blue mermaid-style sheath gowns covered with glittering beads and sequins.
- Add matching long-sleeved jackets.
- Have bridesmaids carry long-stemmed crystal roses.

Flower Girl

- Choose a dress with a full opalescent white skirt with vertical ruffle trimming.
- Accessorize with white tights and white patent leather shoes.
- Top her head with a white fur-like hood hat tied at her chin with a silk ribbon.
- Give the flower girl a white teddy bear or polar bear to carry. Attach a silk drawstring pocket to the bear. Place artificial snow in this pocket, and have the flower girl scatter the snow along the bridal aisle.

Ring Bearer

- Dress the ring bearer in a white tuxedo.
- Have the ring bearer carry the rings on a white velvet pillow. Glue crystals and clear faux gemstones to the top of the pillow for an added sparkle.

Ceremony

Wedding Site

Hold the wedding at an ice skating rink, or transform a hotel ballroom or event site into an ice palace.

Decor

Cover the site with glimmering fantasy:

- Hang a wintry mountain-scene mural on one wall.
- Drape the other walls with sheer white fabric. Create a translucent and enchanting setting by up-lighting the wall with soft blue lighting. Hang twinkle lights behind the fabric.
- Group white evergreen trees around the room. Hang mostly white, with some blue, twinkle lights on the trees.
- Drape the bridal table and the wedding arch with tulle. Place twinkle lights under the tulle.
- Set out metal-frame figures, such as deer, angels, and so on, and trim them with twinkle lights.
- Hang mirror balls above the dance floor and throughout the room.
- Decorate bar areas to resemble igloos.
- Build a skating rink, and construct fake snow piles around the rink. Consider having the wedding party skate out on the ice for the ceremony.

Music

Play chime music, and hire a harpist to perform for the ceremony.

Special Touches

Give guests clear ball tree ornaments. Choose plastic ones that come apart at the seam, and fill them with artificial snow. At a designated time, have guests throw the snow on the couple, instead of throwing traditional rice or birdseed. Large, white paper confetti will also work.

Transportation

Let the bride make her entrance in a horse-drawn sleigh (add wheels when there is no snow). You can use the sleigh to give guests sleigh rides during the reception, and to send the bride and groom away to their honeymoon.

Reception

Area Decor

Hold the reception in the same location as the wedding ceremony. In addition to the decorating ideas suggested above, display ice sculptures on buffet tables and around the room.

Table Decor

- Cover tables with white, opalescent, floor-length tablecloths.
- Tie white napkins with double strings of white pearls.
- Make centerpieces from Lucite in such shapes as snowmen, snowflakes, skiers, and so on.
- Place centerpieces on round mirror tiles, and surround them with votive candles.
- Illuminate centerpieces with blue glow sticks.
- Sprinkle imitation snow on tables.

Favors

- Small, crystal figurines in white gift boxes placed at each place setting

Guest Book

Place the guest book on a clear Lucite lectern stand.

Entertainment

Create a snow-carnival atmosphere:

- Have people dressed as a snow queen and king greet guests.
- Hire additional walk-around entertainment, such as a pirouette mime, a juggler, and a clown. Make sure that all entertainers are dressed in all-white costumes, and that all their accessories, such as balloons, balls, and so on, are also white.
- During the reception, play romantic, classical waltzes.
- Set up carnival games. Select or create games and game pieces to fit a white or crystal theme. Toss dimes into crystal goblets. Toss Styrofoam "snowballs" through white-painted tires. Throw darts at white balloons. Throw white hoops around white stuffed animals.
- Set up a white or clear fortune-teller tent, complete with a crystal ball. Have the fortune teller dress in all-white, opalescent, or very light-blue clothing.

Menu

Let it snow an abundance of treats:

- Vendor carts with white-chocolate candy apples, white cotton candy, hot white-chocolate drinks, cappuccino, and so on

- Hot hors d'oeuvres and sparkling champagne served on crystal-looking trays
- A dessert buffet built with mirror tiers (Select a variety of white-colored desserts. Include white-chocolate brownies, miniature coconut cakes, white chocolate, and white-chocolate-dipped strawberries.)
- A few platters of veggies, fruit, and cheese (such as brie and smoked cheddar) to help guests with their sugar overdoses.

Cake

- Top a multitiered white wedding cake with a sparkling cake topper—place a crystal blown-glass wedding-bell figurine inside a battery-operated fiber-optic light bush.

Wedding on the Orient Express

I nvite guests "all aboard the Orient Express" for a progressive wedding dinner party, traveling to destinations of mystery and intrigue. This creation is set in the 1940s, when wedding engagements were often rushed as men went off to war. However, the setting varies within this progressive event—the wedding party will travel to at least three different-themed destinations, making stops in China, England, and Spain. If you like, you can design your own destination stops, choosing favorite international, intergalactic, or time-period destinations. Wouldn't it be fun to plan stops in prehistoric times, the 1920s, and maybe the space-age future? Or you may want to choose stops made on the original Orient Express: Istanbul, Milan, and Paris.

Invitations

Attach luggage tags to invitations, or write invitation details on the tags. List the date and time of the wedding and reception as follows: "The Orient Express Wedding Train will depart Grand Central Wedding Station at (time) from (place)."

Guests' Dress

Ask guests to wear their traveling clothes. If your wedding is formal, suggest formal attire for the wedding, and ask guests to bring traveling clothes for the reception. If you like, suggest that guests wear traveling clothes from a bygone era.

Wedding-Party Dress

Bride
- Choose a tailored suit.
- Complete the look with 1940s-style ankle-strap, open-toed shoes and a small powder-puff or tailored, brimmed hat.

Bridal Bouquet

- Carry gloves, a leather box-like purse, and a simple bouquet of fresh flowers.

Groom

- Dress the groom in a classic forties-style suit—double-breasted with broad shoulders, wide lapels, and cuffed slacks.
- Add a bold-looking forties-style executive hat and a floral boutonniere.

Groomsmen

Dress groomsmen similarly to the groom.

Bridesmaids

- Dress bridesmaids in red satin oriental-style, knee-length dresses.
- Have them peek over decorative oriental fans.

Flower Girl

- Dress the flower girl in a pretty print dress.
- Have her throw rose petals from a very small hatbox.

Ring Bearer

- Dress the ring bearer in a train conductor's uniform.
- Have the ring bearer carry the wedding rings in an overall pocket.

Ceremony

Wedding Site

Choose an appropriate embarking area:

- If possible, hold the wedding at a train depot, or even on a train.
- Transform an event room into a train depot.

Decor

- Set up a ticket counter, an embarking area, and a waiting area.
- Hang travel posters on the walls.

Music

Play forties-style music. Add travel songs, such as "Sentimental Journey" and "Chattanooga Choo-Choo."

Special Touches

Give toy train whistles to guests to blow at the appropriate time.

Guest Book

Have guests sign a vintage piece of luggage. They can write directly on the luggage, or on make-shift travel stickers made from peel-off sticky paper.

Transportation

- Take guests on a train ride.
- Transport guests during this progressive dinner event in chauffeured limousines, or designate car pool drivers.
- For large groups, lease a bus, or buses, to help keep guests together during the progressive dinner.

Reception

Area Decor

Once guests have boarded "The Orient Express Wedding Train," take them on a progressive dinner party. Travel to various destinations of mystique and intrigue. Set up different destinations for hors d'oeuvres, main course, and finally, dancing and wedding cake. These can be actual separate locations or different food stations within one event site.

For example, perhaps you'll hold the wedding ceremony at a train station or at a park displaying a parked train engine. The first stop during your progressive dinner may be the train station lounge, where you will serve drinks and hors d'oeuvres. Next, you may chauffeur guests to your favorite restaurant for a seated main course. Finally, you may transport guests to a ballroom or event site for cake, champagne, and dancing. A progressive dinner takes a lot of coordination and you will need help to direct guests and to coordinate details.

If you like, decorate each site or food station as an international destination. For example, the first stop's decor may be reminiscent of China; the second, of England; and the last, of Spain. Create your own destinations by working with the site's chef or choosing sites around your city.

(For example, if you have a favorite Indian restaurant, India can be one of your stops.)

Following is a sample three-stop event:

Stop #1 China: Hors D'oeuvres

Decor
- Decorate the area with Chinese room screens, scrolls, paper lanterns, and fans.
- Use Chinese vases as centerpieces.
- Create flower vases from Chinese takeout cartons.

Entertainment
- Arrange a short Chinese-acrobat performance.

Menu
- Mini egg rolls, sweet and sour pork, crab and cheese fried wontons
- Chinese tea

Favors
- Chopsticks tied together with silk ribbons and inscribed with the bride's and groom's names and wedding date
- Personalized fortune-cookie favors, available commercially

Stop #2 England: Main Course

Decor
- Hang up a backdrop of an English pub.
- Set out a red English phone booth for photo opportunities.
- Hang a large British flag on the wall or from the ceiling.

Entertainment
- Have English bobby characters greet guests.
- Play the British national anthem in the background to welcome guests.
- During and after the meal, play Beatles tunes, and provide a small dance floor for dancing.

Menu

- Fish and chips (French fries) with malt vinegar and salt (Wrap the fish and chips in newspaper.)
- Yards of ale

Favors

- Miniature British flags

Stop #3 Spain: Cake and Dancing

Decor

- Create a "fan"-ciful area of Spanish mystique with Spanish-villa-architecture facades, complete with water fountains.
- Accent the room with pepper trees, and scatter preserved leaves on the floor.
- Use torches and plenty of candlelight to create a romantic ambiance.
- Cover tables with deep-red, floor-length tablecloths, and top with black lace.
- Create two kinds of centerpieces: matador hats filled with fresh fruit, and black fans accented with red carnations.
- Lay red roses across black lace fans placed as decorative wedding favors at each place setting.
- Paint gold numbers on green leaves to use as seating assignments.

Entertainment

- Have conquistador-costumed greeters meet guests at the entrance.
- Kick off the cake cutting ceremony with a parade of fruit flambé by the waitstaff. Serve the flambé with the wedding cake.
- After the cake cutting ceremony, entertain guests with a flamenco dancer's show.

Cake

- Decorate a large tiered cake with a Spanish lace fan cake topper.

Favors

- Miniature briefcase hatboxes and suitcases, available commercially
- Lace fans

Arabian Nights— A Wedding of Middle Eastern Mystique

Travel to an Arabian gambling den hidden in a desert oasis for a romantic moonlight wedding filled with intrigue and nightlife fun. This theme is easy to create, and the memories of this unique wedding celebration will linger for a lifetime.

Invitations

- Send a casino poker chip or a pair of dice with each invitation.
- Attach a note: "To enter the Arabian Gambling Den reception, you'll need the secret password—'camel.'"

Guests' Dress

Suggest traditional formal attire.

Wedding-Party Dress

Bride

- Choose a silk taffeta white sheath gown with a wide, pearl- and silver-sequin-trimmed strapless neckline.
- Drape the bodice with the same silk taffeta material and tie it in back with a butterfly bow.
- Top the ensemble with a silver tiara, to shimmer in the moonlight.

Bridal Bouquet

Select an olive-leaf branch for the bridal bouquet.

Groom

Clothe the groom in a black tuxedo and a silver turban.

Groomsmen

Dress groomsmen similarly to the groom, but have them wear white turbans.

Bridesmaids

- Dress bridesmaids in black, straight, sleeveless gowns with empire waists and slits on both sides of the skirt, just below the knee.

  - Have bridesmaids carry silver vases with single roses.

Flower Girl

- Dress the flower girl in a sapphire-blue, A-line, sleeveless, satin dress with a mock turtle neckline. Trim the neckline and the hem with rhinestones and shiny sequins.

- Have this precious flower girl scatter rose petals from an imitation brass bowl or tray. (You can use an authentic brass container, but the imitation is lighter.)

Ring Bearer

Dress the ring bearer in a black tux with short pants, and have him carry the rings in a velvet "loot" bag—a small sapphire-blue velvet pouch gathered at the top with a drawstring.

Ceremony

Wedding Site

Hold the wedding in a large tent.

Decor

- Post a guard at the tent entrance. Have "terrorist-looking" characters meet guests at the tent entrance. They should demand the secret password from all who request entrance into the gambling den. Dress the "terrorists" in men's business suits and desert headdresses. Make the headdresses out of squares of cloth, and secure them with headbands. Add dark sun glasses and toy machine guns.

- Layer the floor of the tent with Persian rugs and large velvet and satin cushions.

- Place large bowls of fruit around the room, directly on the floor near the cushions.
- Line the tent walls with sheer draping.
- Place palm trees around the room.
- Accent the room with brass and metal Middle Eastern decorations.

Music

Play recorded Middle Eastern music, or hire a Middle Eastern musical ensemble. Contact a local belly dancer entertainer for sources.

Special Touches

Throw colorful poker chips up in the air once the couple has been pronounced husband and wife. Be careful not to throw the chips *on* anyone.

Transportation

- Bring the bride to the tent in a black stretch limousine. Provide an escort of two "terrorist-looking" characters. (See Ceremony/Decor for terrorist-looking costume suggestions.)
- Have the wedding party ride to the wedding on camels. Later, entertain guests with camel rides and photo opportunities.

Reception

Area Decor

Hold the reception in the wedding tent.

Table Decor

Decorate small cocktail tables with a combination of casino nightclub accents and Middle Eastern flair:

- Cover tables with white linen tablecloth squares.
- Drape Middle Eastern-print scarves over the tables. If such scarves are not readily available, Indian-print scarves will serve the same purpose. These scarves look dramatic whether used alone or on top of white linen cloths.
- Set simple votive candles on small brass trays in the centers of tables. Provide a place to collect these centerpieces if the tables have to be cleared for card playing.

Favors

- Playing cards printed with the wedding couple's names and wedding date

Guest Book

Have guests write their names on a large, overstuffed floor pillow. The couple can use this pillow as a decoration in their home.

Entertainment

- Hire a casino company to set up game tables, such as craps, twenty-one, and roulette.
- Organize card games at the various tables.
- In one corner of the room, place a small platform for belly dancers.
- Provide camel rides and photo opportunities for guests.

Menu

Set up a Middle Eastern hors d'oeuvre buffet. Additionally, have waitstaff serve a few hot items from silver trays. Guests can eat at small tables or while reclining on pillows. Following are some Middle Eastern favorites:

- Mini gyros
- Small shish kebabs
- Falafel
- Yellow rice
- Fresh fruits
- Olives
- Kibbeh balls with yogurt sauce
- Dolma (stuffed grape leaves)
- Fancy trays of candies, nuts, and figs
- Pita bread
- Baklava

Cake

- Design the cake in the shape of playing cards or a reclining camel.
- Set out an informal sheet cake.
- Bake a traditional, tiered wedding fruitcake. Decorate it with hard candies.
- Serve Arabic coffee with the cake.

Yellow Rose of Texas Wedding Hoedown

K ick up your heels at this BIG Texas-style wedding hoedown. Everything is coming up roses, yellow roses that is, in this romantic wedding done with BIG Texan flair. This grand twist on the traditional barbecue isn't just for summer; this sweet-smelling, romantic event can be held any time of year and will make any bride, Texan or not, a "Yellow Rose of Texas."

Invitations

- Have a printer specially die-cut a very tall invitation.
- Send a long-stemmed yellow rose with each invitation.
- Deliver the invitation, along with a yellow rose, inside a tall cowboy hat.

Guests' Dress

Ask guests to wear yellow and/or western formal wear—modern formal wear (cocktail dresses, tuxedos, formal suits) with western accents, such as fringe, rhinestones, yoke trims, cowboy hats, boots, and so on.

Wedding-Party Dress

Bride

- Choose a rich sophisticated gown for this Texan bride:
  - —Long-sleeved, completely pearl-beaded bodice with a wide scoop neck
  - —Skirt made with soft flowing layers of silk organza
- Complete the look with a layered, floor-length veil held by a wide, pearl-beaded headband.

Bridal Bouquet

Choose a large yellow-rose bouquet.

Groom

- Dress the lucky groom with tall Texan charm in a western-style black silk tux.
  - Add a silk single-string tie, black cowboy boots, and a tall, black cowboy hat.
  - Add a yellow-rose boutonniere.

Groomsmen

Dress groomsmen similarly to the groom.

Bridesmaids

- Dress bridesmaids in black halter-style gowns with standup collars trimmed with sparkling silver bead and sequin trim.
  - Add long, black, silk gloves and small yellow-rose bouquets.

Flower Girl

- Dress the flower girl in a ruffle-trimmed ankle-length dress topped by a white pinafore.
- Place a garland of yellow roses on her head.
- Give her a light, large (about thigh- to waist-high, depending on the age of the child) yellow wreath to carry.

Ring Bearer

- Dress the ring bearer in black jeans, a belt, a white shirt, and an imitation-cowhide vest.
- Have the ring bearer carry the rings inside a black hat.
- Have the ring bearer clang a bell while walking down the aisle.

Ceremony

Wedding Site

- Hold the ceremony in a house of worship.
- Hold the ceremony on a ranch, or create your own "Ewing-style" ranch atmosphere.

Decor

Cover the area with yellow-rose splendor:

- Decorate with an abundance of yellow-rose floral arrangements.
- Cover a heart-shaped lattice wedding arch with yellow roses.

Music

Play the song "Yellow Rose of Texas" at the ceremony. Hire a fiddler to play the wedding march.

Special Touches

Place fresh or silk yellow-rose petals in several black cowboy hats. Ask guests to reach into these hats for a handful of rose petals to throw on the happy couple.

Transportation

Rent convertible Mercedes Benz automobiles to transport guests to the reception site.

Reception

Area Decor

Add Texan charm to the area:

- Hang large, tall murals of Texan landscapes, oil wells, state maps, and historical figures on walls.
- Display tall mural photos of the bride and groom as children.
- Decorate the room with railings, hay bales, bleached cattle skulls, and horse saddles.

Table Decor

- Cover tables with cowhide-design tablecloths.
- Use white wooden chairs.
- Place yellow-rose floral arrangements in black cowboy hats and boots. Accent centerpieces with silver horseshoes.
- Place black napkins with single yellow roses at each place setting.

Favors

- Packets of yellow-rose seeds tied with yellow satin ribbons (Write a table number on the back of each packet. Give these to guests as table assignment cards.)
- Small yellow-rose plants wrapped in silver florist's paper

Guest Book

- Make a very tall guest book or sign-in sheet for this Texas-tall wedding.
- Cover a guest book with imitation cowhide.

Entertainment

- Hire a square-dance caller to lead and teach guests square dancing.
- Have a deejay spin country and western tunes.
- Rent bull-riding and calf-roping interactive game machines.
- If possible, hire *Dallas* TV show look-alikes to greet guests.

Menu

Naturally, this theme wouldn't be complete without a very large Texan barbecue spread:

- Steaks, ribs, chicken, and chili
- Miniature corn on the cobs
- Baked beans, potato salad

Cake

Make a grand Texan statement with the wedding cake:

- Have a baker make a Texas-tall, multitiered wedding cake, each tier a different flavor. Trim the cake with yellow roses.
- Add several large sheet cakes to the table, as well.
- Place yellow-rose-shaped candy mints on silver trays.
- Make large yellow-rose and boot-shaped iced sugar-cookie favors for the cake table. Place the cookies in clear corsage bags, and tie with yellow satin ribbons.

Boston Tea Party Wedding

ere's a wedding party brewing with historical romance. Set in colonial times, this theme wedding is flavored with the pioneering and independent spirit of the American people who began a new life in a then-foreign land. The theme is especially appropriate, since the bride and groom are also about to begin a new life together in new surroundings.

Invitations

- Attach decorative tea packets to invitations.
- Send tiny wood crates of tea packets with invitations.

Guests' Dress

Enclose the following note with invitations: "Hear Ye! Hear Ye! Come dressed in early-American costumes."

Wedding-Party Dress

Bride

- Rent an early-American costume, or design your own:
  - —White silk brocade gown with a wide hoop skirt
  - —Tight-fitting bodice with an open square neckline
  - —Bows and rushings trim (a double ruffle) on the bodice, neckline, and overskirt
  - —Overskirt divided over a decorative petticoat, which is trimmed with two rows of rushings and bows matching those on the bodice and overskirt
  - —Sleeves fitted to the elbow, where a large flowing ruffle is attached and accented by another bow
- Accessorize with a three-row pearl choker and a cameo brooch worn on the bodice.

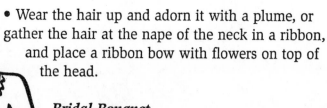

• Wear the hair up and adorn it with a plume, or gather the hair at the nape of the neck in a ribbon, and place a ribbon bow with flowers on top of the head.

Bridal Bouquet

Attach a floral display to a lace fan. Include a stalk of corn in the bouquet—this was customarily done to wish the future husband a plentiful crop.

Groom

• Rent the groom's costume or design one yourself:

—White silk or brocade knee breeches

—Blue waistcoat

—Long full-skirted black or navy coat, worn open, with buttons sewn down one side of the entire coat, stopping at the hip

• Complete the ensemble with a double-layer lace-ruffle neck cloth, black tricorner hat, white socks, and tall, black buckle shoes.

Groomsmen

Dress groomsmen similarly to the groom, but without the full-skirted coat. Choose a different color, such as green, for the waistcoat. Add a powder horn, worn over the shoulder.

Bridesmaids

• Design bridesmaids' gowns to resemble the bride's, made with blue brocade.

• Have bridesmaids carry china or copper teapots filled with floral displays.

Flower Girl

• Dress the flower girl similarly to the bridesmaids. Design her dress short enough to reveal ruffled pantalets.

• Add a colonial ruffle cap to complete the look.

- Give the flower girl a doily cone filled with flower petals to drop along the aisle.

Ring Bearer
- Dress the ring bearer in a Paul Revere-type costume.
- Have the ring bearer carry an early-American lantern with the rings attached.

Ceremony

Wedding Site
Hold the ceremony in a historical site of worship.

Decor
- Decorate pews with early-American lanterns (metal boxes—with cutout windows—which hold a single taper candle).
- Set up a black iron wedding arch.
- Place a British flag on one side and an American flag on the other side of the wedding party. (Historically, the American flag did not yet exist, but allow yourself artistic license to show that Americans were between England's rule and their own independence.)
- Hang early-American lanterns from the wedding arch.

Music
- Hire a drummer to lead the wedding procession with pomp and parade.
- Follow the drummer with a costumed flutist playing "Yankee Doodle Dandy."
- Have a professional musician or group give a bell-ringing performance.

Special Touches
- Shoot confetti cannons filled with red, white, and blue confetti and streamers.
- If the wedding is held indoors, give guests small wooden crates marked "tea." Fill the crates with red, white, and blue confetti to throw on the wedding couple. Have costumed actors representing colonial-era Native Americans lead guests in this effort.
- If you have the ceremony or reception on a boat, fill small wooden crates with colored red, white, and blue sugar for guests to throw overboard.

Transportation

Transport the bride and groom to the reception site in a horse-drawn wagon.

Area Decor

Hold the reception on a boat, at a nautical-theme restaurant, by a pool, or recreate your own early-American ship atmosphere:

- Set up a wooden-plank entrance, wooden tables and benches, ship's wheel, compass, nautical accents, and so on.
- Add large burlap bags and crates marked "tea."

Table Decor

- Cover tables with alternating red, white, and blue tablecloths.
- Make centerpieces of pewter pitchers or teapots filled with red, white, and blue flowers.
- Use early-American lanterns as centerpieces.

Favors

- Commemorative pewter coins, inscribed with the bride's and groom's names
- Hand-dipped candles
- Chocolate tea cups and saucers
- Lobster bibs imprinted with the bride's and groom's names

Guest Book

Have guests sign a "Declaration of Love." Print "Declaration of Love— [bride's name] & [groom's name], [wedding date]" at the top of a sheet of parchment paper. Place the parchment on an antique wooden table, complete with a quill ink pen, pretend inkwell, and a variety of antique books. Have a costumed town crier stand nearby, ringing a handled bell and crying, "Step over and sign the declaration of love!"

Entertainment

- Have greeters dressed as Native Americans and colonials meet guests and direct them to their tables.

- Showcase a short waltz performance, with dancers costumed in early-American clothing. Later, teach guests a few waltz steps.
- Combine historical and modern dance music throughout the event.
- Include marching lessons and musket drills.
- Hold a potato sack race.
- Finally, for a spectacular display, shoot fireworks to celebrate the special day.
- Place the bride's garter around a red ear of corn and hide it in a huge pile of yellow corn. Encourage the bachelors to find the red ear. According to custom, whoever finds the red ear gets to kiss anyone he chooses.

Menu

East Coast delicacies are appropriate for this New England theme:
- Lobster
- Crab cakes
- Boston baked beans
- Parker House rolls
- Choice of iced or hot steaming tea

Cake

- Place sparklers in the wedding cake.
- Serve Boston cream pies.

Tropical Wedding Splendor

T he ocean winds blow lovingly over this island-like wedding of romantic enchantment. Invite friends and family to a wedding luau filled with tropical splendor and romantic island fun. This theme wedding is designed as an artistic interpretation of a tropical wedding (not as an exact representation of Hawaiian tradition) and can be hosted as a casual or formal affair.

Invitations

- Send formal invitations along with coconuts or Hawaiian leis.
- Write invitation details on scrolls, roll them up, and place inside plastic, corked bottles.

Guests' Dress

Ask guests to come dressed in island wear.

Wedding-Party Dress

Bride

- Choose a shoulderless and backless white sarong gown, crisscrossing on the bosom of the dress, and wrapping around the neck.
- Add a detachable floral train to the gown, secured at the waist. To create a floral train, sew flowers closely together onto netting.
- Complete the tropical look with a floral wreath for the hair and a floral anklet bracelet.

Bridal Bouquet

Have the bride carry a floral lei, which she can later place around the groom's neck during the wedding ceremony.

Groom

Choose a white tuxedo with a Hawaiian-print cummerbund and bow tie. Have the groom also hold a floral lei to place around the bride's neck during the wedding ceremony.

Groomsmen

Dress groomsmen in white tuxedos with short pants and Hawaiian-design cummerbunds and bow ties. Have them wear white knee-high socks with white tuxedo shoes. (If the wedding is held on a beach, the entire wedding party can go barefoot.)

Bridesmaids

Have bridesmaids wear long Hawaiian-print halter dresses. Accessorize with tropical-bloom ankle bracelets and floral wreaths, or tropical flowers tucked behind one ear.

Flower Girl

- Dress the flower girl in a grass skirt.
- Add a flower wreath for her hair.
- Have this aloha flower girl carry a coconut filled with flower petals to drop along the aisle.

Ring Bearer

- Dress the ring bearer in a white short-pant tuxedo.
- Add a Hawaiian-print cummerbund, bow tie, and ring pillow.

Ceremony

Wedding Site

Hold the ceremony on a beach, or create your own beach indoors.

Decor

Create a romantic island ambiance:

- Hang up a South Seas beach mural.
- Line a sandy beach with tiki torches to form a wedding aisle. If necessary, create your own stretch of beach by spreading a layer of sand over a plastic or fabric sheet.

- Accent the area with parrots and other exotic birds.
- Add totem poles and torch lights.
- Set up tiki huts for serving drinks.
- Decorate with tiki statues, plenty of palm trees, and plants.
- Create floral arrangements with giant birds of paradise and other tropical flowers.

Music
Hire Hawaiian musicians to create a romantic tropical ambiance.

Special Touches
- Blow conch shells to announce the beginning of the ceremony.
- Give guests floral and shell leis. Have them put the leis on each other after the bride and groom exchange their wedding kiss.

Transportation
Carry the bride and groom to the reception area on bamboo chairs.

Reception

Area Decor
- Hang thatched roofing and/or brightly colored canopies over the bar and food buffet areas.
- Cover buffet tables with grass skirts, and accent with bright Hawaiian-print tablecloths.
- Illuminate pathways to buffets with hurricane lamps.
- Have the waitstaff dress in formal beachwear: rolled-up tuxedo pants, tuxedo shirts, bow ties, and white aprons. Have them go barefoot!

Table Decor
- Cover tables with white linens, add hurricane lamp candlelighting, and place outdoors under the canopy of nighttime stars.
- Drape tables with bright Hawaiian-print tablecloths.
- Place votive candles inside hollowed-out coconuts, and group several coconuts together for centerpieces. Accent with sea shells.
- Decorate pineapples with tropical flowers as centerpieces.

- Make centerpieces by securing an abundance of mango leaves upright inside low, decorative containers.
- Write guests' names on mango leaves, and stick the leaves upright (using floral pins) into oranges, apples, or other fruit to make place cards.
- Make fun island hors d'oeuvre trees. Using toothpicks, cover pineapples with olives, peppers, cheese, fruit kebabs, and so on.
- Use large leaves as place mats and serving-tray liners.
- Serve drinks in pineapples and coconuts.

Favors
- Macadamia nuts in decorative bottles or bags

Guest Book
Cover a guest book with palm leaves.

Entertainment
- Produce a traditional hula and fire dance show.
- Hire a teacher to instruct guests in a hula dance. Provide grass skirts.
- Hold a Hula-Hoop and limbo contest.

Menu
A traditional pig luau, with a pig roasted underground, would be the perfect choice for this wedding. Look in the *Yellow Pages* under Hawaiian entertainment, or contact your caterer for help. In addition, consider the following:
- Seafood crepes and crab salad served in avocado shells (These make nice hors d'oeuvres.)
- Food decorated with edible flowers
- Bottled beers, wine coolers, and other beverages served from ice-filled steel tubs decorated with grass skirts
- Rum drinks in coconut glasses

Cake
- Decorate a coconut cake with tropical flowers.
- Serve the cake with macadamia-nut cookies.

Showboat Wedding Serenade

Invite guests to your own showboat wedding theater, modeled after the river steamships of the late 1800s that carried a theater and a troupe of actors to southern river towns. Warm up the occasion with southern hospitality and a dinner-theater atmosphere.

Invitations

Create an invitation to resemble an old-time playbill listing the players (the bride and groom) and the play's title ("Showboat Wedding Serenade").

Guests' Dress

If you like, ask guests to wear vintage Victorian costumes from the late 1800s.

Wedding-Party Dress

Bride

- Choose a ball gown of southern elegance reminiscent of the Civil War era:
  —Bare-shouldered bodice with a wide single-ruffle neckline
  —Full, bell-like sleeves
  —Large hoop skirt covered with rows and rows of ruffles
- Complete the look of southern romance with a romantic veil or a large brimmed hat and veil, lace mittens (which leave the fingers bare), and a cameo and velvet choker.

Bridal Bouquet

Create an elaborate bouquet with beautiful southern azaleas.

Groom

- Dress this southern gentleman-groom in a double-breasted ivory frock coat with a short waist and a long skirt, trousers, lapeled waistcoat, and high-collar shirt.
- Finish the ensemble with an ascot tie, a plantation hat, a tapestry vest, a cane, and gloves.
- Give him an azalea boutonniere to wear.

Groomsmen

Dress groomsmen in Confederate-gray uniforms.

Bridesmaids

- Dress bridesmaids in southern hoop-skirt ball gowns, each a different color.
- Have them carry matching frilly and open parasols.

Flower Girl

- Dress the flower girl in a dress with a plaid, collared bodice and a hoop skirt short enough to show her eyelet-lace pantalets.
- Give her a single rose stem (take the thorns off beforehand) to carry, and tell her to pluck one petal off at a time to throw upon the bridal path.

Ring Bearer

- Clothe the ring bearer in a short open jacket over a waistcoat and a standup collar shirt with a fold-over tie.
- Place the rings inside a top hat, and have the ring bearer carry the hat down the aisle.

Ceremony

Wedding Site

Decide whether you want to hold the wedding ceremony in a place of worship or on a stage, as part of the showboat "entertainment." If you decide for the latter, see Reception/Area Decor for decorating ideas.

Decor

Decorate the place of worship or the stage area with showboat romance:

- Display large baskets of azaleas, magnolias, and other southern flowers near the alter or another focal point of the ceremony.
- Put oil lamps on large wooden columns.
- Place a large ship's wheel at the center of the area.

Music

Include organ music for the ceremony, and maybe a violin solo. You may also play recordings of Oscar and Hammerstein's *Showboat* tunes.

Special Touches

- Give guests flowers to throw at the bride and groom after the wedding vow exchange. Inform guests beforehand to shout exclamations of "Encore! Bravo!" as they throw the flowers "on stage."
- Design the wedding program as an old-fashioned theater playbill.

Transportation

Transport the bride and groom to the reception and away from the wedding celebration in a horse-drawn carriage.

Reception

Area Decor

- Hang backdrops of a riverboat steamship, a theater stage, and a grand antebellum southern mansion. If you use a stage as the focal point of the reception, alternate these scenes with the entertainment.
- Shine gobo lights on the wall of a riverboat steamship. Hire a specialty lighting company to create the illusion of water waves.
- Set up separate door-sized paintings or posters of the "actors"—one of the bride and one of the groom—at the "theater" entrance.
- Set up an easel with a red velvet marquee in an antique-looking gold frame. Attach photographs of the "actors"—bride, groom, groomsmen, bridesmaids, flower girl, ring bearer, parents, grandparents, and so on. Place a large fern next to the easel, and light with soft uplighting.
- Set up a vignette of a large southern porch with rocking chair, hanging ferns, potted plants, table with serving tray, lace afghan, and so on.

- Set up another vignette as a theater box office window reading, "Show 25¢."
- Decorate the bar area with an antique bar, round wooden tables, and rounded open-rung chairs. Have the bartenders wear costumes: lapel vests over white blouson-sleeved shirts with sleeve garters. Place oil lamps, empty whiskey bottles, and stacks of poker chips on the bar as centerpieces.
- Decorate a stage with old-fashioned velvet curtains and rising and changing vintage backdrops. Add old-fashioned footlights to the front edge of the stage floor.

Table Decor

- Set up round tables in front of the stage for a dinner-theater atmosphere.
- Drape tables with pom-pom-fringed tablecloths.
- Use oil-lantern centerpieces. (You'll have to get permission for this from your site manager.)
- Create playbill centerpieces with a photo of the bride and groom.

Favors

- Flower corsages (for female guests) and flower boutonnieres (for male guests)
- Pralines wrapped in cellophane and tied with pretty ribbons

Guest Book

Invite guests to sign a large scrapbook (guest book) with pages adorned with newspaper clippings, publicity photo shots, pressed flowers, and old playbills.

Entertainment

Provide show-stopping entertainment and melodrama for the wedding reception:

- Start with a parade led by a marching band and followed by the "actors." Hand out helium balloons to guests as you pass by.
- Take Polaroid photos of guests in the southern porch vignette. (See Reception/Area Decor.)
- Hire professionals to write and stage a short melodrama, casting members of the bridal party (be sure to include piano music for this). You can even include family members as part of the cast.

- Have professionals coordinate some additional acts as well: a cancan dance review, a comedy act, and so on.
- Hire a piano player (in costume) or a player piano.
- As a fun mixer, give each guest a playing card, and instruct them to team up with four other players to form the best five-card poker hand. The winning team is given a prize. If you like, tell the players that they may exchange their card once, and set up a special area for the exchange.

Menu

- Southern delicacies, such as gulf shrimp, southern-fried chicken, hush puppies, and so on
- Mint juleps from the bar

Cake

- Serve a large coconut cake and some miniature pecan-pie tarts with lemonade and iced tea.
- Create a fish-shaped cake.

Chapter Three

More Storybook Themes

A Wedding on Easter Day

How beautiful the day that is touched by love. Invite your guests to join you as you exchange wedding vows on this joyous Easter day. Easter bonnets, bunnies, and egg hunts are the theme for this celebration. Send invitations in Easter baskets. For delightful place cards, write guests' names on pastel-colored eggs.

Game of Love: A Sports Fan's Wedding

Touchdown, ace, home run! We've won in the game of love. Invite guests to your "Big Game" wedding celebration. Place invitations inside empty tennis ball cans. Or, write, "You're Invited" directly on a tennis ball. Suggest that guests wear their favorite team's colors. Dress the wedding party in team T-shirts.

Romancing the Wedding

Invite guests to join this romantic adventure in search of the jewel of love and happiness. Model this wedding after the movie *Romancing the Stone*. Conduct a treasure hunt for the "stone," a jewel of love—plan for some rocky roads and adventure. Tell guests to dress casually and to bring snake repellent. Have guests sign a guest book made from a large, wall-sized treasure map.

Calypso in the Caribbean: A Wedding at Pirates' Cove

Ask guests to join you for a swashbuckling pirates' bash under the Caribbean stars. Send a pirate's eye patch or an antique-looking treasure map with the wedding invitation. Hold the wedding on a beach, at an aquarium, or in a nautical-style restaurant. Entertain guests with Calypso music. Blindfold the bride and groom and have them walk the plank, while showering them with rice or birdseed. Later, distribute foil-wrapped chocolate coins from a large treasure chest. Send the wedding couple off in a rowboat.

Tying the Knot at Dixie's Truck Stop

"Breaker, Breaker! Billy and Cindy tie the knot at Dixie's Truck Stop." Hold this fun and unique wedding at a truck stop or diner. Write invitations on blue paper plates, announcing the blue plate special. Or, attach licorice ropes tied into a knot, and announce that the couple will soon tie the knot. Ask guests to bring canned goods or nonperishable food items to donate to charity. Paint "Billy and Cindy Tie the Knot" on the side of an eighteen-wheeler semitrailer. Also print this slogan on large buttons for guests to wear.

"Prisoners of Love" Jail House Rock Wedding

The bride and groom are Prisoners of Love in this rockin' wedding celebration. Celebrate with such rockin' tunes as "Jail House Rock," "Prisoner of Love," "Chains," "Chain Gang," and so on. Lock guests behind bars to make photo favors. Help the lovesick inmates with a breakout escape plan. Stick a large metal-looking file into the side of the wedding cake.

Wedding in Wonderland

Step into the storybook land of *Alice in Wonderland.* Enjoy an afternoon wedding tea with Alice, the Mad Hatter, Jimmy & Lisa, and other characters from the pages of this enchanting tale. Invite guests to wear a variety of hats at this "mad-hatting event." Play croquet with mallet handles decorated with pink flamingo heads. Decorate the croquet course with oversized toadstools and playing cards. Place pole signs on the course, reading "This Way," "That Way," "Which Way," "Right Way," and "Wrong Way." Invite guests to help paint roses on a large wall mural. Serve tea in teapots decorated with "Drink Me" signs.

Chocolate Wedding Safari

Plan a safari to tame the Chocolate Beasty. Enjoy an evening of delectable chocolate treats and the fascinating sights and sounds of the African Wildlife Kingdom. Dress the wedding party in safari garb. Give guests safari pith helmets and toy binoculars. Serve a chocolate dessert and concoctions buffet, including chocolate fondue, chocolate-covered potato chips, chocolate cheese, and other chocolate delicacies. Decorate tables with animal shapes made from imitation fur. Hide stereo speakers in the jungle brush and play animal-noise recordings. Pour champagne into chocolate toasting goblets. After the toast, take delectable bites out of the goblet.

Catch-a-Rising-Star Wedding Ball

Decorate the area with sparkling star decor. Hang twinkle lights from the ceiling to resemble a galaxy of stars. Cover tables with glittering star confetti. Use battery-powered star napkin rings, available commercially. Entertain guests with a star-studded performance. Lower a Marilyn Monroe impersonator from the ceiling on a swing. Give guests autograph books as they arrive. Encourage guests to acquire the autographs of Hollywood celebrity look-alikes.

Halftime Wedding Happenings

Write invitation details directly on footballs. Hold the ceremony on a high-school football field. Have a marching band perform and a cheerleading squad lead guests in a wedding cheer. Give guests pom-poms, team banners, and other stadium souvenirs to wave. Inscribe souvenirs with a wedding day message.

The Big Splash

Throw a pool party wedding reception. Ask guests to wear party attire and to bring their fishtails (swimsuits). Set up umbrella tables next to the pool. Create underwater table centerpieces: Secure gardenias or other large flowers on the bottoms of large clear globe bowls, then add water and a goldfish. Decorate the reception area with mermaid and King Neptune foam core cutouts. Conduct an underwater treasure hunt. Hold a pool toy race.

Blue-Ribbon Country Fair Wedding Celebration

Send guests blue prize ribbons with the wedding invitations. Decorate tables with blue-and-white gingham checkered cloths. Tie yellow napkins with raffia bows, and attach cookie cutters to the raffia napkin rings. Label homemade jars of jam with the bride's and groom's names, cover the jars with country gingham cloth and ribbon bows, and hand them out as wedding favors. Instead of having a dollar dance, auction off homemade cakes, cookies, and pies decorated with prize ribbons.

Isn't It Ducky? Wedding Party

Send guests a yellow rubber duck as the invitation. Hold the wedding at your local duck pond. Feed the ducks and hold your own rubber duck race. Decorate tables with delicate lace tablecloths. Tie matching napkins with yellow satin bows. For "ducky" centerpieces, float yellow rubber ducks in large crystal bowls. Set out a yellow rubber duck at each place setting. Number the bottom of each duck and conduct prize drawings throughout the event. For the wedding meal, serve, what else?—roast duck.

An All-Star Wedding Game

Baseballs or boxes of Cracker Jack make perfect "take me out to the ball game" invitations. Have costumed concession vendors stroll through the crowd with neck-strap vendor boxes filled with baseball-game favorites, such as popcorn, peanuts, and hot dogs. Fill miniature plastic batting caps with bubble gum, and have guests toss the bubble gum near the bride and groom after the ceremony. Make place cards out of ribbon-wrapped Cracker Jack boxes or Babe Ruth candy bars. Invite guests to "catch the baseball fever" with an informal softball game, or rent a batting cage or a softball dunking tank.

Off We Go into the Wild Blue Yonder

Passengers, fasten your seat belts. Flight attendants, prepare for takeoff. Now, off we go into the wild blue yonder of love. Fold invitations into paper airplanes or send toy, balsa-wood airplane invitations. Hang large foam core airplanes from the ceiling. Have a Red Baron character greet guests at the "cockpit" entrance. Hold a paper-airplane making contest. Give guests luggage tags containing table numbers as seating assignments.

Monkey Shines Wedding Party

Take the wedding party to the zoo for this light-hearted celebration. Cover tables with jungle-print cloths. Make centerpieces using baskets of bananas. For table assignments, give each guest a banana printed with a corresponding table number. Have a costumed gorilla hand out chocolate-covered frozen bananas. After dinner, have standup comedians entertain guests.

From Russia with Love

Invite guests to this Russian-flavored wedding celebration. Send an embroidered brocade scarf filled with Russian tea cookies along with a love-letter invitation. Dress the bride and groom in Russian dress. For the groom choose loose-fitting trousers, embroidered tunic, heavy woolen double-breasted vest, belt, and a military-style hat. For the bride choose a Russian folk dress made with embroidered brocade, an apron, and a traditional Kaluga headdress. Recreate a Russian tea room and serve Russian tea sandwiches, tea cakes, and hot steaming tea. Send guests home with personalized bottles of vodka.

Wedding, Hollywood-Style

Action—roll-it! This Hollywood-set wedding catches that star-struck love moment. Send a movie video case with a photo cover of the bride and groom. Inside the cassette case, place a note that says, "You are invited to appear . . . ." Hold this wedding in a makeshift warehouse "sound stage" or on a stage at a local theater. Decorate the area with movie clapboards and movie cameras placed on tripods. Outside, roll out a red carpet and shine a roaming spotlight. Have guests make their own star hand- or footprints in plaster of Paris, complete with autographs and a brass star. Frame the creations and give them to guests as wedding favors.

Bewitched with Love

Conjure up a unique Halloween wedding. Send invitations attached to pointed black witch hats. Make "Wicked Witch of the West" centerpieces: Place a witch hat over a pair of stuffed red-and-white-striped stockings. Add a broom and an empty pail. Show *Bewitched* TV episodes on monitors around the room. Put champagne bottles on ice inside large black cauldrons. Decorate short brooms with inscribed ribbons, and give them to guests as wedding favors.

Wedding "Fan"Tasies

Celebrate this "dream come true" wedding with fondue "fan"tasy. Print decorative Oriental fans with invitation details and enclose small fondue tradition cards that read, "If a lady drops a piece of food in the fondue pot, she must kiss the gentleman nearest her. If a gentleman drops a piece, he must pay for the wine." Decorate the room with various sizes and styles of fans. Place fondue pots on small tables covered with beautiful Oriental scarves. Fold napkins into fan shapes. Serve cheese, meat, vegetable, caramel, chocolate, and other fondues. Have guests cook their own fondue pieces, going from table to table for variety. Give guests chocolate Hershey's Kiss favors. Wrap a few kisses in layers of billowing tulle and tie each bundle with a romantic ribbon.

Sail Down the Nile Wedding

Sail down the Nile to the queen's favorite nightspot. Enjoy an evening of ancient libations, food, and fun. Paint the walls with hieroglyphics. Decorate the area with mummies, sphinx masks, and Egyptian art. Place "elixir" bottles on tables as centerpieces. Dress the waitstaff in Egyptian costumes. Serve Egyptian (or Egyptian-sounding) hors d'oeuvres and drinks, such as mummy meatballs, King Tut tater skins, and mini Anthony's pizza pies. Offer the queen's favorite Nile drinks: hieroglyphic highballs, sphinx sours, cryptic collins, and bottles of Nile water.

Wedding at the House of Bouffant

Hold this sixties cocktail party reception in a beauty shop. Send curlers, combs, or hairbrushes with the invitations. Spin sixties tunes and take photos of guests sitting in hair-dryer chairs. Dress greeters in vintage beauty-shop uniforms and have them carry trays of bite-sized Velveeta and SPAM. Include trays of Hostess Twinkies and Snowballs, cut into bite-sized pieces. Have beauty operators style guests' hair into teased bouffant styles.

Space Station Wedding Stopover

Journey into the galaxy for this futuristic wedding celebration. Send invitations through e-mail or attach space-food packets to the invitations. (You can usually find these at history museums.) Have a set designer create a space tunnel entrance. Decorate the room with neon wall hangings. Set out neon-top tables, available commercially, or cover tables with silver-foil space blankets. For another fun tablecloth option, paint tablecloths with glow-in-the-dark paints. Use neon centerpieces or make centerpieces out of rubber monster masks, stuffed and mounted on acrylic bases. Invite guests to enter transformation booths, and transform them with neon-colored punk wigs, glow-in-the-dark face paints, and glow-in-the-dark painted T-shirts. Shine black lights around the room to illuminate these creations. Give glo-necklaces and Milky Way candy bars as wedding favors.

"Dessert" Wedding Island Delirium

Have an actor dressed in a hula costume personally deliver a coconut or pineapple with each wedding invitation. Have him or her perform a short hula dance for each guest. Decorate the wedding and reception area in tropical island splendor. Set up several dessert buffets, overflowing with delectable desserts, to send guests into delicious "dessert" deliriums. For instance, have a chef prepare chocolate cake, fudge delight, lemon meringue pie, cherries jubilee, cookie-dough ice cream, and so on. Get the idea?

Wedding at the High Hat Club: A 1940s Reminiscence

Envision an Art-Deco glamour wedding at the High Hat Club. Invite guests with re-created Western Union telegrams, or deliver invitations in black top hats. Decorate the room with large, ornate copper vases filled with cala lilies, and line the room with live palm trees. Add Art Deco wall panel facades accented with romantic wall sconces. Encircle the dance floor with swag railings. Place small cocktail tables in the middle of the room. Cover the tables with white linens and small cocktail lamps. Have a cigarette girl and a Philip Morris-type bellman greet guests. Entertain guests with big band sounds and an old-fashioned radio show. Have a roving photographer take photos.

Supplier Resource Directory

Work with wedding vendors (caterers, bakers, entertainers, decor companies, and so on) to create special theme accents for your wedding. Go to the library and explore costume, historical, and classic books. (Tip: Don't forget the children's section.) Classic story and historical videos from your library or local video store are also good sources of ideas for theme details.

To acquire theme-wedding supplies, consider a variety of sources. Visit a costumer or bridal fashion store. Inquire with your local theater to rent decor or costumes. Visit party supply stores and party rental stores for just the right theme design supplies. Shop for theme-related supplies at stationery, gift, discount, department, retail outlet, and specialty stores. More and more theme-related items appear daily on the market. Use your imagination to adapt everyday items to your theme. Also, search for hard-to-find items at antique stores, estate sales, auctions, thrift stores, garage sales, and flea markets. You might even find that perfect theme accent in Grandma's attic.

An increasing number of event vendors supply their products and services nationally, and I have collected a treasury of theme-related event mail-order vendors and services. Some products are only available in large quantities, by the dozen or case. These quantities usually complement wedding-sized needs and often offer you the opportunity to purchase the items at wholesale cost. For ease and convenience, contact your local retail store first to purchase the product. If they do not carry the product, call the listed manufacturer to find out where the product is retailed near you. If you find no local retailers, consider asking your local party supply store, party rental store, florist, wedding coordinator, or other wedding vendor to order the product for you. The vendor may choose to charge you an additional service fee or add-on price. Negotiate the terms with the vendor beforehand. Now, explore the following resource directory for products and services that will help to make your theme wedding event a success.

Costumes

Miller Stockman

Address: P.O. Box 5407 T.A., Denver, CO 80217

Phone: (800) 688-9888, (303) 428-5696

This company's catalog offers a wide selection of western wear and western-related products.

Rose D'zynes, Historical Wedding Attire

Address: P.O. Box 498, Vista, CA 92085

Phone: (800) 899-ROSE (899-7673)

Web site: www.rosedzynes.com

This designer offers custom-designed wedding gowns and wedding party attire, available for sale or rental. The company specializes in historical weddings and covers many periods, including Medieval, Victorian, Roaring Twenties, and others. This designer's creations will also be in bridal shops soon.

Sat'n Spurs Western Wear, Inc.

Address: 6452 E. Hampden Ave., Denver, CO 80222

Phone: (303) 757-7787

Web site: www.satnspurs.com

This western boutique offers western bridal and formal wear, including handmade custom-designed hats and jewelry. Wedding accessories and supplies, including western-design cake tops, invitations, and garters, are also available. Visit their Web site or call for a catalog.

Sheplers, Inc.

Address: P.O. Box 7702, Wichita, KS 67277

Phone: (800) 833-7007

This company claims to be "the world's largest western store and catalog." Call or write for a catalog of western wear and products

Theme Decor

Accent Annex

Address: 1120 S. Jeff Davis Pkwy., New Orleans, LA 70125-9901

Phone: (800) 322-2368

This is your one-stop Mardi Gras shop. They have all kinds of Mardi Gras decor items and other supplies, including beads, doubloons, music, and umbrellas.

Anderson's School Events

Address: 4875 White Bear Pkwy., White Bear Lake, MN 55110

Phone: (800) 748-7004

This catalog is a treasure-trove of decorating kits and decorating supplies for theme events.

CA Corman & Associates, Inc.

Address: 881 Floyd Dr., Lexington, KY 40505

Phone: (606) 233-0544

This company has "face-insert" life-sized photograph panels for any theme. These panels are great not only as decor accents, but also provide a fun activity.

Engineered Plastics

Address: 211 Chase St., Gibsonville, NC 27249

Phone: (336) 449-4121

This company sells illuminated tabletop buffet serving units, bowls, serving trays, and ice-sculpture molds.

Fancy Faces

Address: 73128 Highway 1077, Covington, LA 70433

Phone: (800) 752-3480, (504) 893-2652

This company manufacturers beautiful ceramic masks, jewelry, wall plaques, napkin rings, place-card holders, tote bags, Pat O'Brian Restaurant hurricane glasses, and so on. The products are great for Mardi Gras and other theme parties. The masks make elaborate centerpieces when placed on Lucite stands and decorated with feather plumes, pearls, and tulle. Their all-white centerpiece design is especially stunning and is available for sale or rental.

Flora-Lite Company

Address: P.O. Box 4119, Clearwater, FL 33758

Phone: (800) 411-7381, (813) 443-0369

This company sells battery-operated lights to brighten up floral arrangements, bridal bouquets, cake toppers, and so on.

Golden Age Productions

Address: 2760 Michigan Ave., Suite 2, Kissimmee, FL 34744

Phone: (407) 944–4401

Web site: www.goldenage-prod.com

Golden Age provides quality, low-priced suit-of-armor costuming and props.

In-Touch Creations

Address: 32 Avalon Rd., Hewlett, NJ 11557

Phone: (800) 541-6188

This company makes an elegant table assignment easel. Guests' names and table assignments are listed with a calligraphy font on parchment paper, which is then placed in a beautiful gold frame.

N&N Productions

Address: 5540 High Rock Way, Sparks, NV 89431

Phone: (702) 355-9080

This company offers brass, custom gobo templates at less than half the cost of most competitors. These plates fit over projection lamps to create oversized thematic images on walls, ceilings, and so on.

Neon USA

Address: 5681 Selmaraine Dr., Culver City, CA 90230

Phone: (888) NEONUSA, (310) 394-8814

Web site: www.neonusa.com

The "King of Neon" designs and produces neon centerpieces and props for rent. This company will ship neon cacti, flamingos, or star centerpieces and other props directly to you. They also have some beautiful illuminated light boxes and tables to create "ice-looking" or wedding-white decor.

Specialty Linens International

Address: 2696 Lavery Ct., #4, Newbury Park, CA 91320

Phone: (800) 959-8033, (805) 375-3795

This company sells unique, round tabletop covers shaped to resemble sport balls, including soccer balls, tennis balls, baseballs, golf balls, and others. They also rent more than sixty theme-print tablecloths, such as cowhide print, zebra skin print, and so on.

Specialty Wines, Inc.

Address: P.O. Box 20272, Rochester, NY 14602

Phone: (800) 724-6263

This company offers single-serving splits (187 ml) of champagne or juice, personalized with a custom label and message. These make memorable wedding-day keepsakes. Decorations for bottles are also available.

Sukey Hughes

Address: Route 19, Box 110FH, Santa Fe, NM 87505

Phone: (505) 989-4649

This artist paints oil portraits of the bride and groom in Renaissance costume, using traditional Renaissance painting techniques. She also paints portraits in many other historical styles and periods. Usually commissioned as a gift for the bride and groom, the portraits also make great thematic room decor.

Totally Tubular: Goldman Arts

Address: 20 Flanders Rd., Bellmont, MA 02178

Phone: (617) 484-8842

This company has giant plastic, air-filled tubes that can be hung from the ceiling, wrapped around columns, or wrapped around the outside of the wedding reception building. This is the perfect solution for decorating extra-large areas or creating an extra-large statement.

Victorian Trading Co.

Address: 1819 Baltimore, Kansas City, MO 64108

Phone: (800) 800-6647

This company's catalog offers Victorian items perfect for invitations, table decor, room decor, favors, and more.

Wildfire

Address: 5200 W. 83rd St., Los Angeles, CA 90045-3256
Phone: (800) 937-8065, (310) 645-7787

Wildfire is a one-stop source for ultraviolet (UV) lighting fixtures, luminescent materials, and UV special-effect production services. They have materials to make your decorative props, water fountains, and ice creations glow in the dark.

YAI General Store

Address: 475 Union Ave., Westbury, NY 11590
Phone: (800) YAI-9914, (516) 338-4450

Purchase this organization's creative gift baskets for centerpieces or attendant gifts. They also sell some tapestry/unicorn design address books and other small gifts appropriate for Renaissance-era wedding favors.

Note: Your purchase provides employment for people with disabilities; all baskets are handmade by disabled employees. Sales profit YAI, a health and human service agency serving children and adults with developmental and learning disabilities.

Specialty Catalogs

Back to the 50s

Address: 6870 S. Paradise Rd., Las Vegas, NV 89119
Phone: (702) 361-1950

Here's your one-stop source for fifties memorabilia, including tabletop jukeboxes, poodle skirts, drive-in movie speakers, and more.

Calyx & Corolla

Address: 1550 Bryant St., #900, San Francisco, CA 94103
Phone: (800) 800-7788

Order your floral centerpieces by mail. Beautiful fresh and freeze-dried arrangements will arrive in time for your special day.

The Coca-Cola Catalog

Address: 2515 E. 43rd St., Chattanooga, TN 37422
Phone: (800) 872-6531

Write or call for your catalog of Coca-Cola decorations, memorabilia, and gift items.

Design Toscano, Inc.

Address: 17 E. Campbell St., Arlington Heights, IL 60005
Phone: (800) 525-1233

This company's catalog displays historical European reproductions for the house and garden that are just perfect for theme event decor. You will find an authentic British telephone booth for your English wedding decor, and traditional London bobby whistles for the party favors. Here's a sample of what they offer: centerpiece-sized Italian sculpture reproductions, French art posters, Excalibur swords, Medieval heirloom boxes, Napoleon tapestries, hourglasses, and gargoyle reproductions. And in case you've been looking for a life-sized suit of armor, look no further.

Expressions from Potpourri

Address: Dept. E136-2, 120 N. Meadows Rd., Medfield, MA 02052
Phone: (800) 388-2699

This is a catalog of unique gifts, including green mask hats (perfect for bridesmaids) and lighted angels with trumpets (for centerpieces or other decorative touches).

Hammacher Schlemmer

Address: 9180 Lesaint Dr., Fairfield, OH 45014
Phone: (800) 233-4800

This catalog contains the unexpected, including a Harley-Davidson telephone, night-vision binoculars, and angel light sculptures.

Hanover House

Address: P.O. Box 2, Hanover, PA 17333-0002
Phone: (717) 633-3377

This mail-order catalog carries gifts that can easily be incorporated into theme decor.

Harriet Carter

Address: Dept. 43, North Wales, PA 19455
Phone: (215) 361-5122

This is another source for specialty gifts that can be used for theme decor, centerpieces, wedding favors, and so on.

Lillian Vernon Corp.

Address: 100 Lillian Vernon Dr., Virginia Beach, VA 23479-0003
Phone: (800) 505-2250

This gift catalog contains items perfect for theme decor. For example, camper/miner lamps, available in blue, green, or red, are great decorative touches for a western theme.

Miles Kimball

Address: 41 W. Eighth Ave., Osh Kosh, WI 54906-0002
Phone: (800) 546-2255, (414) 231-4886

Use one or more of the specialty gifts from this catalog as theme decor, centerpieces, wedding favors, and so on.

The Mind's Eye, Memory Lane

Address: P.O. Box 6547, Chelmsford, MA 01824-0947
Phone: (800) 949-3333

This specialty catalog offers recordings of television commercials and TV's greatest hits. Also available: vintage French 1920s-style phones, brass candelabras, class hotel desk bells, original 1940s phones, tie-dye kits, Maltese Falcon statues, train whistles, and lots more.

Norm Thompson

Address: P.O. Box 3999, Portland, OR 97208
Phone: (800) 821-1287

This catalog is an escape from the ordinary with its world of unforgettable gifts. Included are retro 1930s-like phones, chocolate eggs encasing chocolate dinosaurs, many old-fashioned candies, fresh flower centerpieces, and plenty of other unusual gifts with thematic potential.

Past Times, North American Office

Address: 100 Cummings Center, Suite 400, Beverly, MA 01915-6102
Phone: (800) 621-6020

This company offers fine gifts that can be used as perfect theme accents for invitations and thematic decor. For example, you will find Victorian fan cards or Victorian scrapbooks, 1930s radios, Glenn Miller recordings, or 1920s fascinating rhythms, or silver-plated Roman border ewers and fruit bowls.

Personal Creations Presented by Spiegel

Address: 530 Executive Dr., Willowbrook, IL 60521
Phone: (800) 326-6626

This company offers unique personalized gifts great for invitations, wedding favors, or attendant gifts. These high-quality gifts include custom wine bags, private label champagne bottles, custom canning labels, and six-inch fortune cookies containing personalized messages.

Seventh Avenue

Address: 1112 Seventh Ave., Monroe, WI 53566-1364
Phone: (608) 324-7070

This company offers decorative crystal pieces great for theme wedding favors. Designs include tiny gramophones, dolphins, dancing unicorns, and others.

The SPAM Catalog

Phone: (800) LUV SPAM (588-7726)

This catalog contains strictly SPAM logo gifts that make perfect fifties or "artsy" theme invitations or favors.

Walter Drake & Sons

Address: 57 Drake Building, Colorado Springs, CO 80940
Phone: (800) 525-9291, (719) 596-3854

This mail-order catalog contains specialty gifts perfect for theme decor accents, invitations, or favors.

Whales & Friends

Address: P.O. Box 388, Centerbrook, CT 06409-0388
Phone: (800) 234-1022

This is a delightful catalog full of whale and other sea animal gifts that are perfect for decor, centerpieces, and favors.

Wireless, Minnesota Public Radio

Address: P.O. Box 64422, St. Paul, MN 55164-0422
Phone: (800) 669-9999

This catalog offers nostalgic gifts for fans and friends of public radio. It is an excellent source for recordings of masterpiece composers, Celtic music, Broadway's best, and other music and gifts.

Unique Invitations and Favors

America Goes Crackers, Inc.

Address: 656 U.S. Hwy. #1, Pequesta, FL 33469

Phone: (800) 897-1822, (561) 745-5551

This company sells traditional British crackers (small tubes filled with favors) in an endless array of theme designs.

Billian Packaging Corp.

Address: 360 Troutman St., Brooklyn, NY 11237-2614

Phone: (800) 331-1868, (718) 497-5555

Check out this factory's wide selection of "panoramic," total-view stock packaging. These transparent packages are available in different sizes, and can be decorated with hot stamping or silk screening. Fill them with theme-oriented candy or gifts to use as favors or invitations.

Bottle Mailings, a Division of Wilder Ideas

Address: 7790 E. Arapahoe Rd., Englewood, CO 80112

Phone: (303) 741-4050

These unique invitation mailers are clear plastic bottles that come with corks, shrinkwrap lids, and mailing labels. Place your rolled-up message inside the bottle, along with confetti, sand, or other theme-related items. Mail the bottle as is, without an outside container. Look for this product in party or stationery stores. If you can't find it, call to find a retailer near you.

The Butterfly Connection

Address: P.O. Box 1535, Shafter, CA 93263

Phone: (800) 548-3284

Give guests live butterflies in individual pyramid-shaped favor boxes. Release the butterflies after the wedding reception to create a unique memory.

Cookies by Design

Phone: (800) 945-2665

These custom cookie bouquets are perfect for invitations, favors, center-pieces, and so on. They taste good, too! Call for a location near you.

The Crystal Cave

Address: 1141 Central Ave., Wilmette, IL 60091

Phone: (847) 251-1160

This company has a variety of crystal designs, such as ice pieces, roses, cityscapes, and other customized crystal gifts. These pieces make unique invitations, favors, or attendant gifts.

Fancy Fortune Cookies

Address: 6265 Coffman Rd., Indianapolis, IN 46268

Phone: (888) 776-6611, (317) 299-8900

This company supplies flavored fortune cookies with your own personalized message.

First Impressions

Address: P.O. Box 581757, Minneapolis, MN 55458

Phone: (612) 424-9508

Make unique invitations or favors with this assortment of custom boxes, bottles, cans, confetti mailers, envelopes, and tubes. They have boxes that look like books, plastic bottles with corks, cans with money wrapping, foil envelopes, custom fortune cookies, and clear envelopes with confetti.

Forever and Always, Co.

Address: P.O. Box 1605, Syracuse, NY 13201

Phone: (800) 404-4025

These flower seeds will sow an everlasting garden of memories. Each is imprinted with the bride's and groom's information.

Glimmers

Address: 3130 La Selva Dr., #304, San Mateo, CA 94403

Phone: (650) 578-8276

This company sells sparkling (battery-operated) napkin rings and jewelry in a variety of theme shapes. Choose from stars, juke boxes, street cars, cowboy boots, moons, and many others.

Goldman Arts

Address: 20 Flanders Rd., Bellmont, MA 02178

Phone: (617) 484-8842

Check out their funky, inflatable hats! These hats make fun favors, people mixers, or unique centerpieces.

Highsmith Inc.

Address: W5527 Hwy. 106, Fort Atkinson, WI 53538-0800
Phone: (800) 558-3899

Here's an excellent source for ordering empty videocassette, compact disc, and CD ROM cases for making your own novel theme invitations.

Liquid Lights

Address: P.O. Box 2560, Melo Park, CA 94026
Phone: (800) 228-6890

Try this resource for purchasing large quantities of neon liquid necklaces, drink steins, golf balls, and so on.

Moon Publications, Inc.

Address: P.O. Box 3040, Chico, CA 95927-3040
Phone: (800) 345-5473, (916) 345-5473

This is a great favor or invitation idea for a futuristic Year 2000 or Space Station wedding. *The Moon Handbook, a 21st Century Travel Guide* is a travel guide to the moon from a visitor's point of view. The company also sells travel guides to many cities and countries.

Nelson Trading Company, Live Tree Seedling Favors

Address: P.O. Box 85, Central Valley, NY 10917
Phone: (800) 699-1859

This company sells live tree seedling favors personalized with the bride's and groom's information.

Paper Direct

Address: 100 Plaza Dr., Secaucus, NJ 07094-3606
Phone: (800) A-PAPERS

Call for a catalog of unique theme papers, booklet covers, laminating products, and other paper-related products.

Personal Puzzles

Address: P.O. Box 1144, Glen Rock, NJ 07452
Phone: (888) 333-6200
Web site: www.personalpuzzles.com

This company makes crossword puzzles customized to the theme of your wedding. They make great mixer activities, invitations, and favors.

Photonaps, BBJ Boutique Linens

Address: 7855 Gross Point Rd., Skokie, IL 60077
Phone: (800) 722-0126

These cloth napkins are made with a photo design of the bride and groom.

Private Cellars, Ltd.

Address: 2625 N. Chase Pkwy., Wilmington, NC 28405
Phone: (800) 800-4436, (910) 791-1900

This company sells exquisitely decorated private label champagne and wine. The bottles have gold-braided bottlenecks and decorative hot wax seals that can be customized for your wedding.

Professional Marketing Services, Inc.

Address: 1698 Post Rd. E., Westport, CT 06880
Phone: (203) 259-4460

This company has fully operational miniaturized versions of briefcases, hatboxes, and suitcases. Each case is handcrafted by a skilled artisan, using only the finest quality genuine leather. This is a great idea for invitations, place-card holders, and favors.

Romantique Inspirations

Address: 5760 Montessa Dr., Camarillo, CA 93012
Phone: (800) 700-2159

This company has unique foaming-bath powder packets designed to resemble romance novel covers. Each packet is imprinted with a playful story line. These unique gifts make great invitations or favors.

The Rosemary Company

Address: 1244 Windor Ct., Adrian, MI 49221
Phone: (800) 823-3891, (517) 265-3891

This company offers a fragrant and lovely Rosemary for Remembrance personalized wedding sachet.

The Safety Blaster, Corp.

Address: 6532 S. Lavergne Ct., Bedford Park, IL 60638
Phone: (708) 496-8585

Make your next party a blast with this company's confetti blaster party horns, great for nautical themes, Fourth of July, and so on. Salute the bride and groom with this unique item.

Swan Publications

Address: P.O. Box 1455, Plancentia, CA 92871
Phone: (800) 535-SWAN (7926)

This company makes romantic novels customized with the bride's and groom's names—great for gifts, as well as spectacular invitations or favors.

Victorian House

Address: 1203 Columbus Circle, Rm. 333, Janesville, WI 53545
Phone: (800) 597-8378, (608) 758-3050

This company offers beautiful, antique-looking Victorian wedding certificates, wedding programs, place cards, and stationery items.

Windsor Collection

Address: 6836 Engle Rd., Cleveland, OH 44104-4549
Phone: (800) 800-0500

This catalog boasts a jewelry collection with unique theme designs, such as boots, magic lamps, and so on. The brooches make great favors or wedding attendant gifts.

Cakes, Cake Toppers, Etc.

Amazing Cakes

Address: 14934 NE 31st Circle, Redmond, WA 98052
Phone: (425) 869-2992

You won't believe it's a cake. Unusual, show-stopping, 3-D cakes with unbelievable detail. Designs include a castle, Romeo and Juliet's balcony, records, and so on. Words truly cannot describe these creations; call for a brochure. They can ship just about anywhere.

Clergy Services

Address: 706 W. 42nd St., Kansas City, MO 64111
Phone: (800) 237-1922

This company offers a marriage vessel and rose as an alternative to the unity candle. They also have family medallions to symbolize blending families together.

Fellowship Foundry Pewtersmiths

Address: 1605 Abram Ct., San Leandro, CA 94577
Phone: (510) 352-0935
Web site: www.ffoundry.com

This company specializes in Medieval/Renaissance toasting goblets and glasses, cake toppers, and serving pieces.

Gambino's Bakery

Address: 3609 Toledano St., New Orleans, LA 70125
Phone: (800) GAMBINO

This bakery will ship a traditional Mardi Gras "King's Cake"—a cake decorated with purple, green, and gold-colored sugar and containing a plastic baby. They also offer prize T-shirts, Mardi Gras music audiotapes, and Mardi Gras trinkets.

Haydel's Bakery

Address: 4037 Jefferson Hwy., Jefferson, LA 70121
Phone: (504) 837-0190

This bakery will ship a traditional Mardi Gras "King's Cake." They also have a Mardi Gras information booklet, beads, and other related items.

Heirloom Crystal Cake Tops

Address: 4688 8th Ave. N., St. Petersburg, FL 33713-6115
Phone: (813) 328-2222

This company sells solid crystal disks, hearts, squares, and other shapes engraved with the bride's and groom's names. They also have a wedding invitation design. All the pieces make great cake toppers.

Jesters 'n' Jousters

Address: 42 Dollar Rd., Oroville, CA 95966
Phone: (530) 589-4471

Judy Orr designs small doll cake toppers, made to replicate Medieval wedding couples. Working from photos of the bride and groom, she copies the wedding costume, bridal bouquet, and personal features of the bride and groom.

Organic Foods

Address: P.O. Box 24008, Little Rock, AR 72221-4008

Phone: (800) 254-2165, (501) 594-5465

This company ships exotic ostrich tenderloins, steak filet, fajita meat, and pâté. They also carry a full line of wild game, including buffalo, pheasant, rabbit, and so on.

San Francisco Music Box Company

Address: P.O. Box 7817, San Francisco, CA 94120

Phone: (800) 227-2190

Call for a catalog of enchanting music boxes that make unique wedding cake toppers, gifts, or favors.

Entertainment and Other Activities

Bwana Jim—Have Alligator Will Travel

Address: 2284 Deerwood Acre Dr., St. Augustine, FL 32086

Phone: (904) 824-4637 or (814) 697-7781

Bwana Jim will bring alligators and snakes to your theme wedding reception. This unique entertainment will certainly take a "bite" out of your event.

Celebrity Heads

Address: 3751 Environ Blvd., Lauderhill, FL 33319

Phone: (954) 484-7884

This company offers spectacular, larger-than-life, and lightweight replica costume heads of famous people. Turn fantasy into reality! They carry fifty models, including Liz, Burt, Lucy, Sammy, and others.

Classic Fireworks by Events, Inc.

Address: 60 W. Ct., Mandeville, LA 70471

Phone: (800) 783-2513

Put the bride's and groom's names or the wedding theme in lights. Words are magically "written" with fireworks. Entertain your guests with these spectacular indoor pyrotechnics.

Flutter Fetti

Address: 19224 Orbit Dr., Gaithersburg, MD 20879
Phone: (301) 926-4242

This company sells confetti and streamer products. Especially delightful are their small confetti tubes, which make great favors.

Great Pumpkin Carriages, Inc.

Address: 926 N. Topeka Ave., Topeka, KS 66608
Phone: (785) 233-2222

This company rents pumpkin carriages to make your Cinderella event complete. They also supply casino games for home parties and weddings.

Marty Wolf Game Company

Address: 2120 S. Highland Dr., Ste. G, Las Vegas, NV 89102
Phone: (702) 385-2963

Hire a Marilyn Monroe, or other celebrity, look-alike to walk around and entertain your guests.

Maskparade, Custom Life-Size Face Masks on a Stick

Address: Celebration Creations, 7601 W. 101st St., Minneapolis, MN 55438
Phone: (612) 943-2420

Surprise the bride and groom with full-sized photocopy faces of the guests of honor. The faces are mounted on poster board and trimmed with glasses, jewelry, hair, neckties, and so on. These masks also make delightful programs, menus, or table decorations.

A Nite at the Races, Inc.

Address: 3043 Jupiter Park Circle, Jupiter, FL 33458
Phone: (800) 252-7373, (516) 747-3900

Invite guests to put "odds on the favorites." Recreate a "night at the track or races" atmosphere with horse races on video. The company sends you race programs, play money, forms, betting tickets, and so on.

Party Works Interactive

Address: 235 W. Maple Ave., Monrovia, CA 91016
Phone: (888) LAPARTY (527-2789), (818) 305-6655

This company has "larger-than-life" interactive games, such as the human gyroscope, Velcro wall, stand-off joust, and others.

Ragtime-Automated Music

Address: 4218 Jessup Rd., Ceres, CA 95307
Phone: (209) 667-5525
Web site: www.ragtimewest.com

See their solid oak monkey organ—wonderful sound from real pipes! Or check out their pneumatic train whistles. They also have band organ and player pianos. Only available for sale, these items are a bit pricey. But, viewed and compared with other unique entertainment and as a valued wedding keepsake, they might be worth considering.

Song Sendsations, Custom Songs for Special Occasions

Address: Celebration Creations, 7601 W. 101st St., Minneapolis, MN 55438
Phone: (612) 943-2420

This company will write and sing a song parody comprised of personal data as a surprise or as a rousing sing-along tribute to the bride and groom. They'll include an audiocassette, professionally recorded, along with a framed song sheet.

Total Rebound Interactive Games

Address: 6610 Goodyear Rd., Benecia, CA 94510
Phone: (800) 4-REBOUND, (707) 748-0117
Web site: www.totalrebound.com

This company offers spectacular interactive games, such as Clash of the Spheres, Human Bowling, Rodeo Roper, Portable Laser Tag, and so on.

Virtual Reality Productions

Address: P.O. Box 46555, St. Petersburg Beach, FL 33741
Phone: (800) VISUALIZE, (813) 528-1000

Call this company for virtual reality games, such as video surfing or laser gun fighting, to make you feel like you're really there. They'll give you a distributor reference in your area.

Publications to Help with Theme Accents

The "Party" Chest Newsletter

Address: Clear Creek Publishing, P.O. Box 102324, Denver, CO 80250
Phone: (303) 671-8253
e-mail: ccmsparkle@aol.com

Keep up-to-date with the latest party ideas! The "Party" Chest is packed full of new party planning ideas, supplier and service resources, and industry news. Subscriptions include a new theme design with every issue, as well as a theme design catalog. Write or call for a free sample copy.

Party Creations' Book of Theme Event Designs

Address: Clear Creek Publishing, P.O. Box 102324, Denver, CO 80250
Phone: (303) 671-8253
e-mail: ccmsparkle@aol.com

This creative 504-page book is your guide to "unique and traditional theme events with creative flair." It includes complete preplanned theme designs, as well as a myriad of innovative ideas to create your own.

Renaissance Magazine

Address: Phantom Press Publications, 13 Appleton Rd., Nantucket, MA 02554
Phone: (508) 325-0411

A magazine for all who love the Renaissance and Middle Ages. The magazine features articles on costuming, history, castles, jousting activities, reenactments, and role-playing.

Miscellaneous Resources

Association of Bridal Consultants

Address: 200 Chestnutland Rd., New Milford, CT 06776-2521
Phone: (860) 355-0464
Web site: www.bridalbassn.aol

Call them to find a professional wedding planner near you.

The Harry Fox Agency, Inc., A Subsidiary of National Music Publisher's Association, Inc.

Address: 711 Third Ave., NY 10017
Phone: (212) 370-5330

A license is required when recording music to make unique cassette invitations. Contact this agency for forms and licensing information. It's really easy and inexpensive.

Pioneer Balloon Company

Phone: (800) 999-5644

Call them to find a certified balloon artist near you.

Something Old, Something New
by Becky Long

Includes innovative suggestions for everything from invitaitons and programs to decorations and keepsakes; intriguing wedding customs from around the world; original wedding themes; novel suggestions for rehearsal dinners and bridesmaids' luncheons; and a user-friendly reference guide to etiquette and time and money budgeting.

The Best Wedding Shower Book
by Courtney Cooke

This contemporary guide to wedding showers is packed with planning tips, decorating ideas, recipes, and activities that are fun without being juvenile.

The Best Bridal Shower Party Games
by Courtney Cooke

This unique book of party games will get your bridal shower off to a fast and funny start. It contains four group activities plus four pencil games, with duplicate game sheets for eight people.

The Joy of Marriage
by Monica and Bill Dodds

Here is a book of romance and love for married couples. With clever one-line messages, it accentuates the everyday romantic, caring, and playful elements of married life. Filled with beautiful, touching, black-and-white photographs, it's the perfect gift for weddings and anniversaries.

Order Form

Qty.	Title	Author	Order #	Unit Cost (U.S. $)	Total
	Best Bridal Shower Party Games	Cooke, C.	6060	$3.95	
	Best Couple's Shower Party Games	Cooke, C.	6061	$3.95	
	Best Wedding Shower Book	Cooke, C.	6059	$7.00	
	For Better And For Worse	Lansky, B.	4000	$7.00	
	Joy of Marriage	Dodds, M. & B.	3504	$7.00	
	Lovesick	Lansky, B.	4045	$7.00	
	Something Old, Something New	Long, B.	6011	$9.95	
	Storybook Weddings	Kring, R.	6010	$8.00	
				Subtotal	
		Shipping and Handling (see below)			
		MN residents add 6.5% sales tax			
				Total	

YES! Please send me the books indicated above. Add $2.00 shipping and handling for the first book and 50¢ for each additional book. Add $2.50 to total for books shipped to Canada. Overseas postage will be billed. Allow up to four weeks for delivery. Send check or money order payable to Meadowbrook Press. No cash or COD's, please. Prices subject to change without notice. **Quantity discounts available upon request.**
Send book(s) to:

Name_____ Address _____

City_____ State___ Zip _____ Telephone (____) _____

Payment via:

❑ Check or money order payable to Meadowbrook Press

❑ Visa (for orders over $10.00 only) ❑ MasterCard (for orders over $10.00 only)

Account # _____ Signature _____ Exp. Date _____

You can also phone or fax us with a credit card order.

A *FREE* Meadowbrook Press catalog is available upon request.

Mail to: Meadowbrook Press, 5451 Smetana Drive, Minnetonka, MN 55343

Phone (612) 930-1100   Toll-Free 1-800-338-2232   Fax (612) 930-1940